Coun

DARK

When *Dark Estuary* first appeared it was still possible to meet no other gunner on the sea walls of Britain, save perhaps a local fowler. It is a little-known world, the world of tideways where the sea first meets the flat lands of marsh and ooze. It is the private world of the tideline birds, from the little waders which are the most graceful and dainty of all our British birds to the stately wild geese.

In this delightful book, 'B.B.' captures in words some of the magic of the tideways, the shapes and colours of the clouds, the effects of light on the marshes and sea, and the patterns of flighting fowl.

The pressure on the wildfowl population is increasing every year. If the time should ever come when there is no more true wildfowling around the coasts of Britain, 'B.B.' hopes that this book – and its companion *Tide's Ending* – will stand as some sort of memorial and a record of what wildfowling was all about.

'He is one of the most gifted of nature writers'
Ian Niall in *Country Life*

DARK ESTUARY

'B.B.'

Illustrated by
D. J. Watkins-Pitchford

THE BOYDELL PRESS

First published 1953
Revised edition 1980
First published in COUNTRY LIBRARY 1984
by The Boydell Press
PO Box 9, Woodbridge, Suffolk, IP12 3DF

ISBN 0 85115 227 9

Printed in Great Britain by
St Edmundsbury Press, Bury St Edmunds, Suffolk

TO
BILL HUMPHREYS

Contents

The Author wishes to thank the Editor of the *Shooting Times* for permission to re-print 'One Morning Flight' (Chapter 17), and Mr. John Moore for his poem 'Gale Warnings' (p. xi).

Introduction

TWENTY-SEVEN years have elapsed since *Dark Estuary* first appeared and some references in the text will be out-of-date. Where this occurs I have added footnotes. Some of the people mentioned have since died and some species of wildfowl, which were then legitimate game, are now on the protected list.

When *Dark Estuary* appeared as a successor to *Tide's Ending*, it was still possible to meet no other gunner on the sea walls of Britain save perhaps a local fowler. There were still one or two hard-bitten characters, mostly crippled with rheumatism, who made a precarious living from what wildfowl they managed to shoot. But, as a race, they were fast disappearing. It was only on the more remote northern firths that they still plied their punts on the tideway.

I will never forget the scene on one such estuary when I was waiting for geese under a full moon. It was a night of intense frost and a hopelessly clear sky for shooting, with not a wisp of cloud. As I waited on the edge of a dense bed of reeds, a long dark shape came stealing by, reminding me of a crocodile in its noiseless glide. I could just make out the head of the fowler and the movement of his arms as they worked the paddles over the side of the punt for, of course, he was lying full length behind his gun. A bright gleaming spear of light furled noiselessly in the wake of this apparition, a gleam which dissolved as the punt melted out of view. In the distance I could hear the loud clamour of the greylags as they swam along the edge of the shore and it was towards this midnight clamour that the punt was stealthily stalking. Some ten minutes later, there came the roar of the gun, a calamitous sound which was tossed back and forth by the mountains round the bay.

The old punt gunners were a hardy race indeed. Not many made old bones. The notable exception was Selby, Abel Chapman's puntsman, whom I met on Holy Island long before the last war. He was an old man then, near ninety, still fond of the gun but past the rigours of punting.

I have never tried punt gunning. No doubt it is an exciting as well as a dangerous sport and great skill lies in stalking your birds and timing your shot. The freeboard of the gunning punt is virtually only an inch or so and a sudden rise of wind, so common on the northern firths, can very soon spell disaster. Unlike shoulder gunning, there is no actual *aiming* at a bird; the big charge of shot is despatched into the thick of the rising fowl and many have to be finished off with the shoulder gun. This is not always possible on a running tide.

The pressure on the wildfowl population is increasing every year. In addition to the 'marsh cowboys'—the shoot-at-anything-that-moves brigade—many of their favourite haunts are being invaded by oil companies and land reclamation schemes. There are even plans afoot for reclaiming the Wash. I can see the time coming when there will be no more true wildfowling around the coasts of Britain. When that day comes, perhaps this book, and its companion volume *Tide's Ending*, will stand as some sort of memorial and a record as to what wildfowling was all about.

'BB'
Autumn 1979

'GOOD FOWLING WEATHER'

GALE WARNINGS

Draw close the curtains. (Mare's Tails streaking the night sky
        And looks like rain?)
With the wireless going, you won't notice the creeper
        Rat-tatting on the pane.
Shut out the night with its wild whispering voices,
        Its cries and its calls,
The tempestuous world kept at bay with your solid
        Inviolate walls.
So settle down to a peaceful finish to Christmas.
        Kick off your shoes;
Cherry-logs merrily crackling, a drink at your elbow,
        Time for the News.
Cat on the hearth, book on your lap, and suddenly over the air,
        Out of the void, into your quiet,
        Come the great sea-names that roar and riot,
Humber, Lundy, Faroes, Forties, Fastnet, Forth and Finisterre!

Tendril of creeper beats a tattoo on the window
        Like a limed linnet.
Know now that you live on an island!—Your house is
        An island within it!
The pitiless winds of the world all about you; and surging
        Into your room
Comes the heave and the sigh and the crash of the steep Atlantic,
        The spray and the spume.

1. *Between the Tides*

IT is a little-known world, that world of the tideways, where
the sea first meets the flat lands of marsh and ooze. It is not
frequented in the holiday season by trippers. It is the private
kingdom of the tide-line birds, the exquisite little waders which are
the most dainty and graceful of all our British birds (with the exception, perhaps, of some of the warbler family), the numberless
ducks, from trim pintail to portly mallard, and the dignified and
stately wild geese.

A few fishermen know this land, a few 'longshore fowlers, and
bird watchers, and one or two painters who find in those wide
horizons and ever changing colour effects a beauty which is
unknown inland.

To see it at its best one should visit it in the winter, for then the
muds and creeks are thronged with bird life. That is why for me
the English winter has so much beauty. I was talking the other
day with another who holds the same opinions as myself in these
matters. He said that for him the summer was a dull and sleepy
time, that he never really awakened until he heard the far-up
signal cries of the incoming fieldfares, or better still, the celestial
chiming of migrant geese.

Though for me the summer holds much charm, as I shall show
(I am an inland dweller, living as near the centre of England as it
is possible to live), I also feel something stirring in me when the
leaves of autumn fall, a nameless excitement, a restlessness, which
must be faintly akin to that uneasiness or wander pain experienced
by migratory birds. The English winter is to me very beautiful

(though many hate it). The sight of a naked hedgerow, purple, intricate, a tangle of delicate lines woven into a continuous but interesting pattern, gives me great measure of delight.

I like to see the ground ivy, visible now in the seemingly dead season of the year, how it twines and covers the sturdy butts of century-old hawthorns which have been laid again and again by the hedger's hook; I can admire the dead, long grass which fringes the field ditches and whose ashy-buff tint makes such a charming contrast to the purple-bloomed thorns. Here and there a briar hangs over the ditch, studded with glowing hip berries which remain upon their armoured raking branches all winter through. Even in the sombre gloom of November and December days those berries burn brightly as though lit internally with fires.

Upon these briars the bullfinch sometimes sits, and I always fancy that our winter frosts put a more roseate hue into his breast, improving his plumage, much as frosts put a 'snap' and crispness into celery.

Perhaps the bullfinch is the favourite of all my midland birds; there is something so sturdy and John Bullish about his build. He has not the anxious old-maidish expression of the chaffinch, nor has he the latter's timid, trundling gait. He sits 'all square' upon his briar stem and takes life as it comes, and his little devoted wife who is always near is, in her way, just as beautiful in her quiet harmonious greys, blacks, and whites.

I admire the partridge also, a little gentleman to the bone. Like the bullfinch, he is devoted to his mate and is sociable and self-reliant. Even though his world is not of the hedgerow and coppice, there is an individual beauty in his winter surroundings, in the dun stubbles which stretch away into the mists where boundary hedgerows are barely visible in the dull days of winter.

There is something of the wildfowl about the partridge, and that is another reason why I like him. But when from soft October skies there comes down to me the call of the fieldfares as they

2

sweep over in swinging flight, all inland delights are forgotten, my mind is busy with another land, and with other birds, the salt marshes of the East Coast, the remote estuaries of the Highlands.

My purpose in this book is to try and capture some of the magic I have felt on the tideways, to set on record my observations of the birds which people it, a book of pictures both mental and visual. Each scene reproduced is one I have myself witnessed and experienced. It is my habit when on the coast to carry with me a small note-book. In this I jot down the shapes and colours of clouds, effects of light, marsh and sea, the patterns of flighting fowl, and then, while yet the picture is bright in my mind, I make a small sketch from which I later paint the complete picture.

I find that if I can get to work on a composition within a day or so of actually fixing it in my mind, I can, with the help of my notes made on the spot, give a fairly accurate impression of the actual scene.

Most of the loveliest effects are to be seen at dawn or evening flight. The midday hours are not so productive except in wild and stormy weather, with perhaps snow or frost. But dawn and twilight are the magic times, and then the artist and wildfowler can look upon rare beauty which the inland dweller can never know.

I have often wondered which is my favourite time, dawn or evening flight. They are so different. Dawn flight on the coast is, however, usually more exciting. At the moonless periods many of the geese, curlew, plover and gulls flight inland to feed, having slept all night on the high sands or marshes. Gulls on the coast rarely sleep on the marshes in winter; they come in from the pastures at evening and go far out to the sand-banks and when they are flooded off simply rest upon the flowing tide.

Individually, and seen close at hand, all the gulls are beautiful birds. I often think that they have in their admirably simple plumage the colours of the sea; the pure white of the breakers, the grey-blue of the sea, the black of wet rocks and the pinks of the sands. They are completely in harmony with their habitat and suggest that absolute 'rightness' of plumage which we find in the greenfinch. Wordsworth says of the latter bird, "a brother of the leaves he seems", and the same suitability of colouring can be noted in the warblers, green woodpecker, kingfisher and nightingale. In the plumage of the kingfisher I can see the azure glint of summer skies reflected in the gliding breasts of streams and rivers, and its ruddy crest reflects the warm tones of the sandy bank wherein it makes its nest.

It would be hard to find a more suitable plumage for the nightingale, a lover of shadowed groves, even its eggs have a midnight tint. And how right too is the plumage of the wryneck and wood owl, and incidentally how suited is the mournful hooting of the latter in the moonlit woods.

But to return to the sea gulls. Their voices suggest the ancient mystery of the sea, a keening which is born of wind and wave. They are best seen, perhaps, not in the London parks or on the Thames Embankment, nor wheeling and screaming in one con⁄fused mass about the harbour fish market, but on the coast at dawn and evening flight in winter. On the marshes they are usually the first birds to move. I like to see them on a calm morning beginning their procession inland. The common and herring gulls are of sociable disposition and at times observe strict flight formation; they are almost as particular as geese in this respect. This is especially so if their feeding grounds are some way inland.

Like most other fowl at the moonless periods, they spend the half light of dawn in washing and preening and then come off in small trips of six to twenty birds. There is nothing hurried in their flight; they give the impression of being lazy, which indeed they are. Their flight is very restful to watch, a measured, effortless wingbeat, and for the most part they travel in silence, especially when they have some distance to go. Most tide⁄line birds, curlews, gulls, plover and geese, seem to have a very definite goal at morning flight. It may be some pasture away over the mountains, a dozen miles or more. When the growing radiance in the east bids them set out for the day's work there is no wandering up and down the tide-line; each bird knows its destination and for this they steer, silently and with purpose.

But there are times when they are tempted to play, perhaps by some thermal or set of wind. I remember a year or two ago, whilst waiting for geese on the shores of Loch Leven, seeing an impressive display of soaring flight.

There must have been a thermal at a fixed position above the marshes, for hundreds of gulls, I might say nearly a thousand, were attracted to one particular spot and with rigid, outspread wings they began to climb slowly in a vast spiral, wheeling round and round, soaring ever higher until they were invisible to the naked eye. This spectacular display lasted for about twenty minutes to half an hour, and every gull that morning which came off the loch was drawn to that spot. It was sheer joy of flight and motion which attracted them. At times gulls indulge in this aerial display much as buzzards do, and also, I might add, the homely rook. Without effort of flying they can soar to an immense height above the earth, and being lazy birds they revel in this form of play.

These aerial exercises however only take place in open weather when the birds are not hungry. I have never seen it during bitter and continued frost. It is a mark of well-being. That is why rooks are seen to indulge in aerial play during the early and middle autumn months, when they are stuffed with rich fare.

For the gulls the journey back to the sea begins early in mid-winter days. Soon after three o'clock you can see the advance guards coming back and their formations are not so ordered. They come in singly sometimes, or in little bunches, and they twist and turn as they come and are more vociferous. The later parties, however, those from distant feeding grounds, adopt the early morning formations, but all are more noisy; and the same certainly applies to the geese.

It is strange also how sharp-sighted are all gulls on the coast. They seem to me to be as wary as geese and spy a gunner in a dyke with equal cunning, nor will they fly in range, but with a sharp warning 'kee weeze' twist and turn away or sometimes go back upon their tracks. This is curious as they are not shot at on the coast, at least not by professional fowlers; only 'tit shooters' and 'Cockney Tailors' shoot at gulls.

The gull on the coast is a very different bird to that of the Thames Embankment or the London parks. To him man is a potential enemy and he takes care to give him a wide berth.

While I admire gulls individually at close quarters, though their form and carriage are graceful and their plumage exquisite in its simple purity of harmonious tones, they do not attract me as do the geese or even the waders. But I do delight in their morning and evening journeys, for they are part of that magic of the tideways. Without them much of the charm would be lost.

2. *Goose Country*

TO the uninitiated the term 'Goose Country' possibly conjures up wild marshlands miles from anywhere with waving acres of reed and treacherous bog. This, however, is far from the case. I know good goose country at once by the look of it, I had almost said the 'feel' of it. The same, incidentally, applies to localities where rare butterflies are found. I know, for instance, what is good purple emperor woodland even though the butterflies may not be visible. I know what is good large blue country (the large blue is one of the rarest of all our blues and is only found in the West Country). I likewise know at once, by the 'feel' of it, where I might find a red-backed shrike, or a bullfinch, tree pipit, corn bunting, or woodlark. It is a sort of sixth sense which only a naturalist possesses and which only comes with long experience.

The fact is that good goose country is far from wild; it is mostly rich arable land. In Lincolnshire it is those expanses of fertile fields, fields so extensive that you cannot see the boundary dykes. These areas are as vast as the flat acres of sand and ooze which lie over the sea-walls and they are ideal for geese. The wild goose likes as much space around him as he can get. Normally he fights shy of small meadows and keeps well away from ditches and dykes. If only the wild goose had a grain more of intelligence he would never be shot on these tremendous fields. If he made it a fixed rule never under any circumstances to pass within range of the boundary dykes, if he could see more clearly in the moonlight and half-darkness, no goose would ever be shot by a scatter-gun except by unsportsmanlike methods such as digging a pit in the centre of the feeding areas or by camouflaged-grass netting. Not even a goose with a human brain could be safe from the last-named practice. Nor of course would it be safe from the man with a high-powered ·22 rifle.

I say at once that shooting at geese with a rifle is the most heinous of all crimes and is thoroughly unsportsmanlike in every way, and it is a crime which is committed frequently by those who have no real love of wildfowl and wildfowling. Once geese have been shot at with a rifle they will forsake their chosen feeding grounds and will leave the district. They have come to gauge the lethal range of a twelve-bore with a very nice exactitude. A ·22 bullet whining amongst the feeding gaggles is feared as much as a falcon. Like humans, geese fear that which they cannot understand.

In moonlight and half-darkness geese cannot see very much better than a human being. Really they are day-feeding creatures and are driven to night-feeding by persecution. They have found over long experience that as a general rule they are left in peace at night; that is why they choose the full-moon periods for feeding, and sleep during the day.

They are also able to judge with a great nicety the time of moon-rise and moonset. Anyone who has studied these grand birds and has lived in the country where they come each winter will know this. Pinkfooted geese, which travel farther to their feeding grounds than greylags, will sometimes leave the shore when it is practically dark, timing their arrival on their feeding grounds to coincide with the rising moon. How they find their way at night cannot be answered; it is certainly the same instinct which tells them the direction of the migrating high-roads.

In Scotland, good goose country is usually within a dozen or fifteen miles of an estuary or firth. In many of the Scottish localities I have visited it has the same outward appearance, large fields for the most part, bordered with post and wire fences, fences which appear rather flimsy but which are in reality very difficult to negotiate as they are fortified with many strands of barbed wire tightly stretched.

These fences rarely give cover to a stalking gunner. There is sometimes a fringe of dead grass (in winter) which grows all along the bottom of the fence, but it is usually too scanty to give any cover to a crawling man, and one's only chance is a dyke. Some of these fields are dyked across and these ditches are usually quite deep and invariably full of water which is over your waders. Some hardy, young fowlers do not mind water over their waders, but I detest it, indeed wherever possible I contrive to keep my legs and thighs dry. This is not mollycoddling. You will stalk much better if you are warm and comfortable, and in any case it is not worth risking chills and rheumatics on a fowling trip which may lay you up and waste valuable days.

Of course there are times when a wet 'belly crawl' is your only chance of success, but once the stalk is over it is prudent to return to your fowling H.Q. and get into dry things.

It is not difficult to keep dry, either when stalking geese or lying in wait for them. Long, *stiff*, fisherman's waders and mackintosh trousers will look after your legs and thighs and a leather jerkin will take care of your upper anatomy.

These Highland fields are never so extensive as the Lincoln-shire 'flat lands' and, on the whole, there is a better chance for a stalk.

Nearly every Scottish 'goose' field has a dyke somewhere near, if not along the fence, then between the geese and the sea. A gun rightly placed can often get a shot if the birds are skilfully driven, as I describe elsewhere. Dead ground also may be made use of.

9

It is amazing how dead ground exists when at first sight a gaggle seems in a hopeless position. You cannot tell until you are down on a level with your quarry.

Sometimes greylags will choose a small field where the grazing is exceptionally good and where there is even a good deep dyke which will give cover to the gunner. But greylags are at times rather stupid birds, besides being greedy.

It is curious how certain pastures are resorted to year after year by geese whilst others just over the fence are hardly ever visited.

There is another point to bear in mind. Geese are less wary when at feed towards the end of the afternoon. They have their bellies to fill to sustain them all through the moonless nights, which are of fifteen hours' duration in midwinter.

Towards four o'clock on a mild winter's afternoon you may see large gaggles greedily cropping the grass whilst other roving bands, possibly disturbed by farm hands off their chosen pastures, are ever lowering and cackling to join those which have found safe harbour.

At such a time and hour even the pinks throw caution to the winds and pass within range of dyke and fence. They see their companions massed on the grass or stubble and know that all is quiet and safe. So, with bands playing, they drop over the trees, one quick, close circle round and wings go up and paddles drop and with a great cackling of welcome they say 'How-do'.

But watch the skeins come in at dawn, or rather soon after dawn, to their feeding grounds for the day. Many times I have watched them. Lying snugly in the dyke, well screened by bleached grass, one sees the light grow and one's surroundings become plain. The hares are active in the half-light and the partridge coveys begin to creak and move.

Incidentally, talking of partridges, I often marvel how they roost out in the bare stubbles on nights of driving rain. Their feathers are not primed so well as those of waterfowl: how do they manage to keep dry? The roosting habits of these grand little birds are not well understood. I am not sure that on nights of storm and rain they *do* sleep out in the open. I have an idea that they seek the dykes where the grass gives shelter, or maybe the scant hedgerows. This applies to inland partridges as well as those in goose country.

But to return to the geese. When the sun is well up you hear from afar, borne upon the wind, the familiar cry of the skeins. Soon they come swinging in with a loud cackling. Their wings wag slowly as a man rows a boat on a quiet river. They set their great vanes and wheel about, passing many times directly across the chosen field and beating away out of the range of vision. But keep low and do not move your head, still less peer over the rim of the dyke. What those geese are looking for, with maybe a hundred sharp, little, brown eyes, is the small white blur of a human face and the two pale smudges of a man's hands.

If you keep your face hidden and your hands under your chest, they will not see you if you have some strands of dead grass to break your body outline.

Back and forth they wheel and pass, and then, with sudden decision, wings go up, paddles are dropped, and with a great forward fanning of grey pinions the whole gaggle comes to rest. At no time did they pass within range of a dyke or other cover: the descent was made by a series of spiralled steps until every bird is down. Mark now what happens.

All the birds stand erect and motionless like soldiers on parade, their small heads turning every way as they scan their surroundings. Then one bird gives a tentative pluck at the grass and walks a pace forward, to stop again to look and listen and maybe to catch some threatening taint on the morning air, though I do not think their sense of smell is keen.

Within ten minutes of landing all are at feed, moving gracefully forward with a light and springy step, and taking short plucks at the grass. The carriage of the wild goose, both pink and grey, is very graceful, so unlike the pouchy waddle of their farmyard cousins.

One or two birds are always on the watch, usually those on the outskirts of the flank, and few feed for very long without a quick scan of their vicinity. Should the sentries see or hear anything to arouse suspicion, they lean slightly forward and give a low croaking note which has the immediate effect of raising every down-bent, plucking head. If not unduly alarmed, they will slowly walk away from the supposed danger, and if they make up their minds that all is not well, they run forward and take the air with a great outcry and beat away for some other spot well known to them.

Hares will frequently run among the gaggles, but the geese do not heed them unless they think something has alarmed the hare.

When all are feeding contentedly their mood is made audible by the low buzzing sound they make, a contented 'coo'. They buzz like this as they swallow down the tender-grass blades, which gives the sound a peculiar muffled quality, like a sheep 'baaing' with its mouth full.

In the early part of the season, when the birds are less wary, some fowlers decoy them with stuffed geese set up head to wind in the grass or stubble. And against the post and wire fence these locals build 'blinds', wire netting laced with straw or hay. A number of young geese are killed by this method, but the rest soon get wise to it, and by the end of the season decoys are more apt to warn the geese away than to attract them.

3. A Wildfowler's Summer

AS I have said in the first chapter, the English winter is to some a hateful time. For such folk even the autumn is sombre and sad, suggestive of decay and dissolution. But to the wildfowler and, I might add, the fox-hunter, it presents a very different picture.

I suppose I am fortunate in being able to appreciate all the seasons of the year except that short period between the end of January and early March. Perhaps if I were a man of wealth it is then I should leave these islands and seek the sun.

I have little good to say of February. It is neither stark winter nor early spring: a half-and-half month. It is then our bodily health is at the ebb and our powers of resistance low, a time comparable to the 'small hours' of night.

Early March is also somewhat distasteful to me, but I know that the return of the chiffchaff is at hand. Already then the evenings are beginning to lengthen and a certain faint bloom appears along the hedgerows, a bloom like that on a grape, not green, for the buds are still far from bursting, but a certain 'aliveness', a sheen, is visible on the twigs, especially when they are seen from the hedgeside and you look along its length.

But by then the gun is put away in its case: there will be no more shooting until next autumn. I suppose that is a rather typical remark of an English sportsman. The anti-sport clique will say he is never happy unless he be chasing or killing something. But in my case shooting and *watching* (whether I am watching birds, butterflies, or simply effects of light and shade) are all bound up in one another; they add immeasurably to my enjoyment of the English countryside.

With the spring there is boundless interest. The return of the migrants is in itself a never-failing source of intense delight. First the chiffchaff, half-heard on the winds of March; then the tremulous falling scale of the willow-warbler in the woods (and I live buried among woods), and then comes the tranquil April evening, or sometimes late afternoon, when I see the swallows, a pair of them, back on my garage roof. They are weary and silent, but so manifestly happy to be back. Every summer they rear two broods in my garage. They spatter the shining glory of my car with spots of white which, if not removed at once, eat into the cellulose, leaving little indelible patches. But I do not mind. When the garage is closed at night I make sure the window is left ajar so that they can go in and out at daybreak.

When April merges into May, the hunting lust is long forgotten. Each succeeding day is full of interest and charm. The swifts arrow about the evening skies, the bell-like voice of the cuckoo sounds continually from meadow to grove, the blackcap returns to the thickets by my garden pool, and surely no bird song is so full of the joy of life. He bubbles over with it. The whitethroat sings among the nettles which are now so strong, green, and thick; and last of all comes the fly-catcher.

He comes silently, magically. One evening the apple bough above the box hedge is empty, then a casual glance reveals him sitting there like a grave, little, grey image, tail restless, head turning often, and now and again there is a sudden sally after passing gnats and the faint snap of his slender beak. The fly-catcher sets the seal on summer and all the glory of the sun and greenness.

14

Then, in the ripeness of July, there is for me what is perhaps the greatest thrill of my summer.

I live in a county where there are large oak woods, ancient forests where once the kings of England hunted the deer and wolf. There I wander when the July sun swelters, when the meadow-sweet is out in bloom, filling the air with its sleepy feminine fragrance, the time also of the lime scent. This is the hour the forest calls me and thither I go to watch, not birds, nor fish, but insects, the lovely monarch of all our butterflies, the regal purple emperor.

He is, I consider, unique among our butterflies. Though you may consider I have no right to introduce him here in a book which is devoted to winter delights and to wildfowl in particular, I make no apology for his inclusion. I hunt him with the same persistence with which I hunt the wild grey geese, though in this case it is purely for the pleasure of watching him in all his glory.

Regal to look at, he is regal in his habits. For he has his throne, the very top of the tallest oak-tree in his vicinity, and there he sits on his special leaf basking in the hot summer sun, opening and shutting those blindingly purple wings. This purple sheen on his wings reminds me of the new fluorescent paint which one sees on the hoardings—it has a burning brightness. The female, which is much larger than the male, has no purple glory, nor does she spend most of her time on the oak-tree tops. She is of a simple black and white design, but nonetheless very handsome. When on the wing she reminds me of a black and white bird, a pygmy magpie perhaps. Both butterflies have a very swift and powerful flight and are extremely hard to net. This is fortunate as it is a very scarce insect, and that strange race, butterfly collectors, will travel many miles on the chance of procuring a specimen. So I do not intend to give away my own pet oak wood where every year I find it in comparative abundance.

There is a tremendous fascination for me watching these rare butterflies enjoying themselves on a day of high summer. The air is vibrant with the hum of insects, heavy too with the perfumes of the meadow-sweet and oak-leaf. Shadows band the long ridings, the silvery sallow bushes, which are the food plants of the purple emperor, are motionless in the heat.

Then perhaps there is a flash of purple as a male swoops down from the oaks in pursuit of a female. Down the riding they race with great swiftness until maybe he loses her among the sallows.

In the lovely July of 1951, I saw a dragonfly pursue a female purple emperor for forty yards down a riding. Then she turned and chased the dragonfly!

When the afternoon is perhaps at its hottest and it is a relief to seek the cool shade of the sallows, the purple emperors go to rest. Since soon after sunrise they have played and fought in the sunlight, living with gusto each vital second of their brief forest life. But as soon as the sun begins to lower and the shadows lengthen, they seek their rest. With a powerful pair of glasses one can see them crawl along a topmost branch, right in among the leaves, and when they have found a resting place they close their wings and go to sleep.

Memories of good wildfowling days are usually made up of winter storms, snows, frosts, dying light, and the turmoil of the tide-line. But butterfly memories, equally pleasant to recall, are exactly the opposite: always sunny, dreamy summer memories, a different world indeed.

One other hobby of mine carries me on to when the wildfowling season comes round once more, and that again is a totally different hobby, but just as absorbing as the others.

As soon as the fishing season opens in June, I go after the big carp, seeking them in a favourite Lincolnshire lake I know of which is buried among beech woods on a private estate.

The only similarity between carp-fishing and wildfowling is that sometimes the best chances are at night and you have the same vigil in a foreign world of shadow and darkness.

In those beechen woods I have in mind, where the royal ferns grow in huge sheaves, many badgers have their home. Sometimes, as I watch my rod, I hear them grunting and moving in the fern. One night in June 1951, when I was fishing this same lake with a friend, a badger came and routed in his knapsack which was doing duty as a pillow. From all accounts the surprise of both parties was mutual.

The very big fish do not begin to move until after midnight at midsummer.

In the half-darkness the white candles of the chestnuts rise tier upon tier to the luminous sky. It is not usually cold in mid-June. You can 'bivouac' quite comfortably with a sleeping bag, and your hand is ready to grasp the butt of your rod.

As soon as midnight has passed, heavy plunges sound on all sides, now here, now there, and ripples come rocking along the bank. The carp in this lake run very large, up to 20 lb. It is difficult to describe the singular attraction which this midnight angling has for me; it is like no other form of fishing. I have tried for sea-trout in Scottish rivers through many a summer's night and found it exciting enough. But these lone vigils by the tree-shadowed pool on the Lincolnshire Wolds are vastly better.

In sea-trout-fishing there is the continual muted roar of the river to break the stillness, a sound which, at night, dominates everything, even the hooting of owls. But there by the hushed pool every tiniest sound can be heard, the rustle of a moth entangled in the bushes, the furtive footsteps of the night-hunting creatures in the bracken, the secretive sucking of a big fish: the ear and eye is tuned to receive these things, the senses are at a high pitch.

Though I occasionally drop off for a moment or two at some time during the night, I find I sleep like a wild animal with one-half of my brain alert, a primitive sort of slumber and maybe not the most restful.

Towards dawn, when even the fish seem to cease from jumping, I am fully awake again. And the vapours drifting above the pool are very ghostly, assuming sometimes the shapes of ships and galleons, or strange outlandish giants which glide unaccountably across the far end of the water. I usually camp near a small ram under some hazel bushes. The muffled beat of it is like a heart-beat, a comforting, friendly sound.

Soon, over the chestnuts, a curious glow gradually suffuses the eastern sky, and the chestnut spires, which a moment ago were mere dusky, nebulous smudges of white, are revealed, spire on spire, climbing from water to sky. A robin sings suddenly, sweetly, close by among the thickets, and a moment after the first blackbird warbles, and cuckoos call continually. Soon the whole, glad chorus is under way. And there is a new smell in the air, keen and fresh—the smell of the dew of a summer dawn.

These, then, are my other delights apart from wildfowling. Nor are they in any sense stop gaps, a mere filling in of that period between the dates of February and October.

When at last the purple emperors are no more, when their infant, big-headed caterpillars have tucked themselves up for the winter in their cunningly-sewn sallow leaves in the naked winter woods; when the carp have gone down into the mud and the summer migrants have all departed, then I am on the threshold of another winter, another wildfowling season, and the yellowing leaf and clucking fieldfare fill me with new joy. It is the tide-line now that draws me, the lonely foreshore, and the misty firth.

So many interests, so many hobbies . . . yes, indeed, these are the things which for me go to make a full and rich life. The naturalist-sportsman may be a queer bird; I'm not sure, actually, that he is a very common one. There are some that shoot, but who are no naturalists; there are very many naturalists who do not shoot nor fish. For me the combination of the two go hand in hand, each adds enjoyment to the other, and I have mentioned these things to prepare the reader for the chapters which follow, otherwise he might accuse me of being inconsistent. I love the wild goose I sometimes seek to slay as the fox-hunter loves the little red fox he hunts.

But there is something else beside all this. The scene, the hour, the time and place, all play their part. Unlike fox-hunting, the sport of wildfowling (and I might add the study of butterflies, bird watching, and carp-fishing) are best sampled alone, without any companion save perhaps a dog.

And now it is time I got back to the silvery tide and the thin clamour of wildfowl, borne on the wind of a winter's day.

4. Puddy Tat Hill

THE long winter of 1950–1 was a dreary time. It began with frost and snow in early November and continued right on until, virtually, the end of May.

With so little sun and so much cold, harsh weather, illness was rife, and when I went down with influenza just before Christmas it left me very run down. Even the prospect of going north in early January did not fill me with the old enthusiasm, but I knew this was only a lowness of spirit, that when I could get off I should be well again; and so of course it proved.

I was to go with Bill on the 4th of January, meeting Mac with the shooting brake at Grantham on the morning of that day, and going on north with him.

But two unforeseen circumstances occurred to upset our plans. First Bill, ever a reckless driver, took a corner too fast and woke up in Rugby Cottage Hospital. On the 2nd and 3rd, snow-storms swept the Midlands and made travel by road a hazardous undertaking. Frantic 'phoning to the A.A. for road reports gave no cause for optimism: the same intelligence was always forth-coming, "roads over the Pennines unsuitable for motor traffic . . . ice, snow and drifts at Carter Bar".

At the eleventh hour my cousin, Tony Wilson, took Bill's place, and as Mac and I could not pick him up at Grantham he came to me by train and I met him at the station.

I got on the 'phone to Mac in Norfolk and, to my astonishment, he told me he intended to start in the shooting brake whatever the weather. Hang the roads reports! Snow was not lying deep in Norfolk and he thought he could get through. When on the trail of the grey geese, nothing can stop Mac; he is that sort of person. But conditions were different in the Midlands, and Tony and I decided to go by train. On the 4th it snowed harder than ever, and soon after breakfast the 'phone rang. It was Mac. He had reached Holbeach and was pushing on, with conditions getting worse. On the following day Tony and I settled ourselves comfortably in our carriage, and we were soon watching the white landscape with its leaden sky pass in a procession before the steamy windows. Discussing a very excellent roast goose in the dining-car (most appropriate dish for wildfowlers), we speculated where Mac was. Tony, draining his Worthington, surmised he was probably at that moment upside down in a snow drift.

Now I had actually started, the old excitement was rising in me. Every bump of the rails was taking me to the land I loved, to the call of the geese along the dawn tide. The sight of the snow-blanketed Pennines, already half visible in the gathering gloom of the winter afternoon, added a spice to anticipation.

When Tony and I disembarked from the train at the little wayside station, the wan light from the single platform-lamp shone on glistening, hard-caked snow. It also illuminated the broad shoulders of Mac who was waiting to greet us. His journey had been an eventful one. He had made it, but only just. And as we drove away down the road, ice hissing and crackling under the wheels, he told us the latest goose news. He had that evening been down on the shore and had never seen so few geese. Just as I feared, the continued hard weather had driven them away. The prospects were far from cheerful.

Looking again just now at my diary of this trip, I see the same monotonous entries: "Dawn flight at Leaning Buoy . . . hardly a goose on the Firth. . . . Evening flight Curlew Bay . . . three pinks came in fairly early, nothing else moving, more frost last night and the flooded fields are frozen solid."

These frozen, flooded fields presented a unique sight and one which I had never seen before in that locality. During the day-time when the sun shone—and we had much clear, glittering weather for most of our time—miles of flooded land was visible from the high hills to the north of the firth. The dazzle of the sun formed a wide, glittering path on the icy skin which locked plough and pasture alike.

It was our regular procedure each day, after morning flight was over and we had had breakfast, to make a tour of the high ground, scanning the low-lying pastures next the firth for feeding geese. It made me realize how difficult it is for anyone without some means of transport to carry out this routine spying for fowl. If we had confined our attentions and energies to the shore alone, our bag would have been very meagre, apart from much wasted time during the daylight hours.

I would say that no matter what the weather, the daily tour with the telescope is essential if you really wish to get the most out of a wildfowling holiday. We had many farmer friends on those flat lands bordering the firth who were only too pleased to let us have a try at the geese if they happened to be using their pastures.

Though all this glittering icy expanse of flood and the white, crisp grass was attractive to the artist's eye, we saw no sign of geese, only numberless crows, rooks, partridges, and pheasants, and an occasional hare which looked as big as a well-grown dog against the snow.

In normal times when the weather is open, all this ground is real 'goose country', and a tour by 'scouting' car will discover for you many hundreds, sometimes thousands, of geese feeding on their favourite fields. Pinks seem to prefer barley stubble to fresh grass; greylags eat a good deal more grass than pinks. It is strange that the two species do not seem to mix, though I have frequently seen both species feeding on the same field. Usually, however, you will find greys in one field and pinks in another.

The best time for watching the big lots is in the early part of the year, just when they have arrived in late October and November. After that time the big gaggles break up and scatter, though in an open winter on the firth I have in mind one may count on 1,500 to 2,000 geese, pinks and greys mixed, which make up a resident population. The greys are far less apt to wander and do not appear to change their feeding grounds as frequently as pinks. The latter may be here today and gone tomorrow and you cannot count on them with any degree of certainty.

On referring to my note-book, I see that our first morning flight, after a frosty night, was quite mild and a temporary thaw occurred. There was very little moving at morning flight, though I missed a single chance at a greylag which came in to the sea over my head. As I was of course looking the other way, I never had a chance to get the gun up until the goose was well out over the muds.

But that afternoon we had our first exciting moment (date, January 7th). From a mild morning the weather had changed again; the hard times were coming back. A cold mist gathering soon after midday was its advance guard. We were scouting in the van and, drawing a blank at all our favourite fields, we went higher up the firth to hitherto unexplored country. Soon I noticed a small conical hill of stubble on which the snow still lay in patches away to our right. We stopped the van and Mac took a spy through the glass.

I had noticed, with the naked eye, some dark spots ranged along the hill-side and thought they were feeding rooks, but Mac soon exclaimed, "There they are!"

I should say that thirty geese—whether pinks or greys we could not see from where we were—appeared to be busily feeding on the south slope of the hill, and we at once made our way to the farm.

Personally I hate asking for permission from strangers, nor is Tony good at this delicate business. So Mac had to go, as he always does, and after a long interval he returned with a rather dazed expression.

Apparently the door had been opened by a quite ravishing blonde, and a few moments later this lovely lady appeared, driving a large car down the lane. Neither Tony nor I could blame Mac for having a far-away look in his eyes. She had been most gracious and told us we could certainly try for the geese. So it was we were introduced to Puddy Tat Hill (the title will be made plain in a moment), and this locality was to provide us with some exciting times for the rest of our trip.

We left the van in the farmyard where sparrows chirped and the smell of far-off summer still seemed to linger, and walked past the house to spy the land. We found that a narrow and very rutty lane led directly towards the swelling hill, passing a little to its left. This was the obvious course to take and, as we were about to return to the van, a large party of pinks came cackling from the sea. After wheeling several times round the hill, they settled on some flat fields on the left of the lane, about a hundred yards from the hill where the other geese were feeding (or at least we imagined and hoped they were).

These newcomers rather upset our plans and we held a council of war. We decided on the only course open to us. If we walked boldly down the lane, we should at once be seen by the pinks who were now chattering and feeding in the flat, unapproachable field. These geese would rise and give the alarm and take the others with them from the hill.

The only course was to drive the van slowly down the lane and bring it to a standstill behind some straw stacks which were on the left—between the geese and the hill. This we did and, as we drew up behind the stacks, the pinks all lifted with a great clamour and made off. We were sure that the birds on the blind side of Puddy Tat Hill had lifted too, though we hadn't seen them do so. The only thing was to have a spy. We tossed for the chance. Mac won.

We were still a little way from the foot of the hill, so we decided to take the van farther and disembark Mac at the foot of the fence. We slowly moved off. Then a rather surprising thing happened. Over the fence and not thirty yards from the lane I suddenly caught sight of five long necks sticking up like umbrella handles. They were greylags. They had seen and heard the van and were on the point of flight. Mac, with great presence of mind, immediately reversed the van and we gained the shelter of the stacks again without the geese lifting. Greylags will sometimes allow one to do the most outrageous things and they (like big game in a national park) had evidently not connected the van with their deadly enemy.

Mac now got out with his Magnum 12 and, with BB in both barrels, began to squirm back along the lane, keeping close to the fence which was the usual 'goose country' type, post and wire. A fringe of dead grass grew all along the bottom of this fence and the road was slightly below the level of the field. Even so, he had no more than an inch of 'freeboard' and had to keep well down in the melting slush.

In about twenty minutes Mac had wormed a dolorous sixty yards and was almost up to the geese. It was watching him creep-ing along the fence which gave us the obvious title to the hill. Mac was, without any doubt, *Sylvester*, the wicked Puddy Tat of the song (it's probably forgotten now but it went like this, if you remember, "I dort I saw a Puddy Tat a-creepin' up on me, I *know* I saw a Puddy Tat as plain as plain can be. . . . You bet he saw that Puddy Tat, dat Puddy Tat was me!").

At last there came the moment when we saw Mac's booted legs spidering crabwise into the lane. He was pivoting on his elbows for a shot which he took through the wire, one on the ground and one as they rose. Bang! Bang! Mac was up battling with the wire.

One jump and he was over and vanished out of sight over the rim of the stubble. I did not know whether he had scored or not, for I had seen no geese rise. We walked down the lane and Mac's head came bobbing over the hill. Two greylags hung from his left hand, their snow-white sterns together and broad wings flapping wide. It was a good start to the trip and it had been a good stalk too.

There will be many sportsmen who have never chased geese in their lives who will be disgusted at anyone 'shooting sitting'. But the bird is so wary that this is quite legitimate and sometimes it is the only chance you will have of bagging a wild goose. At the end of a stalk you are nearly always in a completely prone position. If you get to your feet, or even your knee, for a shot from behind a fence, the geese will be up and far out of range before you can get the gun to your shoulder.

This then was our introduction to Puddy Tat Hill. We were destined to have other adventures there before the trip was over.

5. Books and Pictures

FROM time to time, usually at the beginning of the fowling season, I pick up Abel Chapman's books and read him with great enjoyment. One of my favourites is his *Borders and Beyond*, wherein he gives accounts of many a day and night in pursuit of wildfowl, mostly along the Northumberland coast. He must have been a very lovable personality and withal a happy man; he always writes with gusto and with such schoolboyish enthusiasm. He was also an artist of considerable ability with an immense knowledge, not only of wildfowl, but of other birds, beasts, and butterflies. He knew a lot about salmon, and was one of the first people to take the trouble to watch their habits at spawning time in the waters of the Houxty burn on his estate in Northumberland.

He travelled widely in many parts of the world: in Spain after the great bustard; Africa and the Sudan, where he shot big game; and he made many journeys to Northern Europe, egg collecting and hunting elk, deer, and boar. Chapman was lucky as he had ample private means. From all accounts he made the best possible use of his good fortune.

He died soon after World War I at a ripe old age and left behind him a mass of literature, much of it of outstanding interest to the hunter-naturalist.*

Chapman was a true hunter-naturalist, the best possible sportsman in every sense of the word, of the same calibre as Selous, Roosevelt (both were of course his contemporaries), Hesketh Prichard, and Millais.

I like his drawings too with their captions such as "The

* Regretfully, many of the authors and artists mentioned in this chapter are now dead

Supreme Moment . . . another ten yards and we have 'em!" or "Hurrah! Ten geese down"—"dark as a dog's throat".

Oh, yes, this is the right stuff! We find the same boyish enthusiasm in Colonel Hawker, though Hawker was a much lesser man and not much of a naturalist.

Only the other evening I was reading Chapman's account of 'a night's flight shooting' where he tells of being abroad in his gunningpunt with his stalwart henchman, Selby. I am always glad that I met Selby on Holy Island between the wars, a fine old bearded character who, of course, told me many things of Chapman. Selby was a great age when I met him, and he must have long since been gathered to his fathers.*

Reading Chapman's descriptions of a midnight expedition on Fenham Slakes, I was reminded of my own experiences, not only on Fenham Slakes and Budle Bay, where at one time I did quite a lot of shooting, but on other places round our shores, both on the east and west coasts.

His books are not now easy to get and should be snapped up whenever the chance occurs. W. H. Riddell illustrated many of his writings. Riddell is sometimes very good indeed. It is surprising that his work is not more widely known, for at times he rivals Thorburn in his bird pictures.

Archibald Thorburn will surely ever be the Audubon of Britain. I have always been a great admirer of his work, and his original paintings now fetch high prices in the sale room.

Yet if one keeps one's eyes open one may still get an original Thorburn for a reasonable sum. In 1949 I managed to get a superb little watercolour of a longtailed tit at its nest in a gorse bush—price five guineas including frame! It is one of his later works but is delightfully done.

'Mac', who figures in these pages, also picked up a magnificent large watercolour of a partridge in the snow for £15. This

28

* Selby died in 1945, aged ninetytwo

is one of the finest Thorburns I know, beautifully fresh in treatment and with charming colour. His oils I do not like so much as he is inclined to overwork them, and if he errs at all it is in making his birds too tidy. His very best work is seen in his sketch-books.

In the early part of his career he published many of his pictures in the old *Strand Magazine*, and I have often wondered what became of the originals. One particular painting I remember was of a brood of partridges, cock, hen, and cheepers, in the lee of some gorse bushes. Thorburn water-colours are still possible to obtain at private sales, and, curiously enough, only last week I heard of an amazing bargain made by a friend of mine.

There was a sale of old silver at Ludlow and included in the sale were fifteen water-colours of birds by Thorburn. My friend heard of this, and, not being able to get there himself, told a friend to bid up to £150 for the set.*

They were some of the original water-colour drawings for Thorburn's best-known work, volume one of *British Birds*. He got the whole set for £45! Each drawing must be worth almost that!

I had the pleasure of looking at these magnificent pictures and I must say that they are far and away better than the reproductions. They are so exquisitely painted it is hard to see just *how* they are done and I found myself marvelling at such skill. Lately I had been looking at the big Holbein in the National Gallery, *The Ambassadors*, and had likewise marvelled at both the drawing and painting of that magnificent work.

Sometimes one can hardly believe the human eye and hand can produce such masterpieces and one is left with a feeling of despair, especially if you happen to be an artist yourself.

Another artist I admire (though not a British artist) is Lilljefors, the Swedish painter. I do not know whether his work is well known in this country, but I have a volume of his paintings which contains some monumental works. In the exhibition of

29

* Thorburn's paintings now fetch very high figures in the sale rooms, and those originals are worth over £1000 each

Swedish art some years ago at Burlington House there was a vast picture of his—a golden eagle swooping on a hare. The eagle was life-size and the picture was hung, if I remember aright, on the wall facing the staircase in Burlington House. It was the first picture you saw as you mounted the stairs, a breath-taking introduction to the exhibition.

Our own artist Frank Southgate, now dead, the East Anglian artist, did some excellent work in water-colour, not only of wild-fowl (Southgate, like Roland Green of our own day, lived among the birds he painted), but of Broadland. No other artist in water-colour has ever recaptured the subtle essence of Broadland as did Frank Southgate. He was a keen wildfowler too.

Charles Simpson, and of course G. E. Lodge have produced fine bird paintings. Lodge is particularly good on the falcons, though with his studies of the smaller birds I think he errs in making the birds' heads too big, a fault which I find with D'Armour's paintings of hunting scenes. His horses' heads and especially the heads of his huntsmen are, I consider, often out of proportion. Seaby is sometimes in the top flight. Peter Scott has produced some fine paintings which, at their best, are almost as good as Lilljefors', notably the Brent geese flying behind a breaking wave, which appeared in *Morning Flight*.

The soundest bird draughtsman today is undoubtedly Tunni-cliffe. He was a contemporary of mine at the Royal College of Art and we studied together in the engraving school whither I gravitated after gaining my diploma in the Painting Schools.

An engraver by nature, his birds are often too static and statuesque and I do not think he is so good at motion. His sitting or standing birds always seem to me more successful. But he at times obtains a rare harmony of colour as well as sound drawing, though, like Thorburn, his birds are apt to be too tidy. Lodge, on the other hand, is inclined to make his birds appear as though they had but lately emerged from a bath.

Talbot Kelly is another talented bird artist with a very individual style of his own. I worked under Kelly at Rugby School, and he taught me a lot about the drawing of birds. He has always been influenced by Egyptian art, for much of his boyhood was spent in Egypt and he has never lost this influence. He is clever at grasping the essential characteristics of a bird and he gets those essentials in a few lines, just as Shepherd—brilliant bird artist in line—could draw a sparrow or a pelican in a few strokes. He was the Phil May of bird artists.

Talbot Kelly works in water-colour helped by a pen line, though he also paints in oils. Latterly he has done some fine work in lithograph, and he is also extremely clever in modelling birds in metal, wood, and paper. Visitors to the Festival Exhibition in 1951 may remember some of these models.

Perhaps the greatest of all bird artists, when he is on top of his form, is the Scottish artist Edwin Alexander, now dead. His water-colours, mostly gauche drawings, are few and far between, and he never seems to have produced very much work. What he did produce is in private collections and is much sought after.

Alexander was a greater artist than Thorburn, immeasurably so. Thorburn was the ideal illustrator for bird books, especially text-books, but Alexander was something more. His paintings have a rare beauty which is missing from the work of any other bird artist living or dead.

Talking of Thorburn has led me away from wildfowling books. I have enjoyed *Marsh and Mudflat* by Kenneth Dawson and, of course, *Morning Flight* and *Dawn Chorus* by Peter Scott (for he writes as well as he paints). *Sport in Wildest Britain* by Hesketh Prichard is another great favourite of mine. When on top of his form, Prichard writes beautifully and manages to convey the atmosphere of that land between the tides better than anyone. J. C. Cornish is another excellent writer, *Nights with an old Gunner* being a charming book.

Sir Ralph Payne-Gallwey's *Fowler in Ireland* contains some excellent material, though it is on the technical side. He was a puntsman rather than a shore shooter.

The tragic death of Terence Horsley in a gliding accident a few years* ago robbed us of a very gifted writer; a real fowler if ever there was one, and a man who could record his impressions in effortless style, full of truth and observation. His *Sporting Pageant* should be in the library of every fowler, if only for the wonderful aerial photographs of many of the Scottish firths I know and love so well.

Wildfowl and Waders by Major Hugh Pollard, illustrated by Southgate, is a splendid book—good writing and fine pictures to match the prose.

Wentworth Day's *Modern Fowler* is another favourite, for he can excite the slumbering lust for the lonely tideway as much as anyone. If only he would restrain himself when he comes to the Viking Hosts and the Long Ships stealing in out of the North! Nevertheless I pick up *The Modern Fowler* many times per year and always lose myself in its pages. Jimmy Wentworth Day always reminds me of a mixture of Cobbett, Colonel Hawker, and Sir Alfred Munnings. I'm sure he won't mind my saying this, for he is a friend of mine and he knows a very great deal about the Essex marshlands and the birds and animals, both human and otherwise, which are found there. I doubt whether anyone living today knows that coast so well, or can write about it with such charm and veracity.

The next best thing to wildfowling is reading about it and looking at good pictures, and another author-artist I shall mention is Millais, whose book *The Wildfowler in Scotland* is in the first flight of good wildfowling books. Millais knew more about ducks, especially the diving ducks, than any of his contemporaries, and he was not only able to write about the sport he loved but also to paint and draw the pictures he saw. Like Chapman, he was

* At the end of the 1940s

fortunate in his birth, for his father was the great Millais, the P.R.A., and he inherited his father's love of shooting as well as painting.

As a small boy he was given great licence and used to wander off with his dog and gun to hunt the wilder bays and coasts of Scotland, being absent from home for weeks at a time. What parent would give such licence now?

Eric Pitman's *And Clouds Flying* is my last choice. Well illus-trated and extremely well written in the Hesketh Prichard vein, it is one of my favourite wildfowling books.

So much for the library and picture gallery. I have not mentioned any of the older writers and artists: St. John, for instance, who was not a particularly good naturalist in that he slaughtered ospreys, but who was one of the first people to write on natural history subjects with any authority: nor have I mentioned any of the older bird artists. The colouring of the old artists' work is beautifully restrained and decorative, but I never really feel their birds are alive, and the legs of the smaller birds are nearly always too thick and clumsy.

Bird photographs have reached such a pitch of excellence that they form a complete section in themselves. Frankly, I have never been enamoured of photographs for book illustration; however beautiful they may be they will never rival the brush of the artist, who has the power of selection both in form, colour, and design.

A Norfolk Bird Sanctuary

IF you look at a map of the coast of Norfolk you'll see, opposite the little village of Morston, midway between Hunstanton and Cromer, a strange rib of land* shaped like the thigh-bone of a man. In some freakish way the sea has eaten round behind it, leaving this natural barrier of dune and shingle. Its name is Blakeney Point: a locality famous for its birds and plant life and the mecca of many earnest students of natural history.

One autumn day my friend Bill and I found ourselves heading for this romantic coast which I had not visited for many years. We drove hour after hour over the flat fenlands, lands which showed on every hand the russets and madders of autumn days, and about the fields lay the sad promises of winter.

A pale sun lighted the first hours of our journey but hateful rain was hard on our heels, and actually it proved to be the wettest week-end of 1950 on the Norfolk Coast.

I enjoyed the changing scene as we went along, and how quickly it does change in the East Country! All the way to Lynn the sky embraces all: you might be upon the flat roof of the world, but once past that quaint and salty township you plunge straight among Norfolk lanes with their hedgerow oaks, big woods, and red-tiled houses and farms.

On the signposts you see the word BY-ROAD. Where these by-roads go to nobody seems to know or bother his head about.

* Much of this was swept away in the disastrous flood of January 31, 1953.

I've never found out. They seem to say, "It's none of *your* business where we go, you keep to the main road!"

The sun had nearly gone when we reached Little Walsingham but its pale reflection glimmered wanly in the diamond panes of a lovely old Elizabethan manor house we passed by the way. Gold horse-chestnut leaves strewed the road; we passed an old Norfolk labourer with faggots on his back. He should have been clad in leather jerkin and high-crowned hat. In the park and gardens we should have glimpsed gentlemen in cloaks and ruffs, ladies in wide, flowing gowns walking among clipped walks of yew.

At last, towards evening, we saw before us, over a ridge, the North Sea, a melting grey line beyond the bar of Blakeney Point. At the little village of Morston we met Ted Eales, the National Trust Watcher, clean-shaven, jersey-clad, ever hatless, his face permanently tanned by wind and weather. Ted's a great chap, keen on his job, knowledgeable too on the sea-birds, a real son of Norfolk moulded by this bleak windswept coast. His father was a coastguard who was watcher on the Point before him. I was glad to see too that he is young and vigorous, and he leads a life many of us would envy. If I was given the choice of a job in a factory at a thousand a year* or Ted's job at Blakeney Point, I know which I'd choose!

We embarked in his motor-boat at Morston Quay, though we had to wait for the tide to flow. At low water there's only a muddy creek which winds away across the marshes, and the Point is three or four miles distant. You can walk across the marshes at low water but it's a weary way and a muddy one, or you *can* go all the way round by Cley Bank, a shingly tramp of nearly five miles.

Our gear was fairly light for we had brought no tent with us. Ted Eales had promised to find us some shelter. Our departure from the quay (a wooden jetty on the marshes) was witnessed by a small group of dogs and people. (The departure of any boat in any part of the world is an excuse for idle interest.)

* Inflation! Five thousand a year is now more like it

As we chugged along the quickly rising water I saw the mud banks sliding past and the withered flower-heads of the sea lavender which were so glad and bright when last I was there in the summer. The change within a short four weeks was dramatic; there was no colour now upon these marshes: they were grey and khaki, the sky was grey, creeks grey, and the sea grey.

When we at last landed on the Point and walked up the dunes towards the watcher's house I saw there *was* colour, after all, in the silvery sand at my feet. Flat rosettes and stars of (to me) unknown plants showed tiny pale-pink flowers, and some of their leaves were stained brilliant golds and carmines against the silvery, warm-toned sand.

Thrift still bloomed and the dark-tinted soueda bushes, which offer such warmth and comfort to the weary migrant birds, made a striking contrast to the pale desert spaces. I was reminded at times of a miniature Arizonian landscape, the dark tufts of soueda became cactus plants, the distant dunes high sandy mountains.

As an emergency measure, Ted Eales had put us in the old lifeboat-house, which is really the headquarters of the London University botanical students, who do much useful work there every summer.

This was a large building with a very cosy, brick fire-place at one end, a book-case full of bird and botanical books, benches, and one long table. It reminded me of the headquarters hut of some exploring expedition, which, in a sense, it is. It was a great boon to us to be able to use this room, though virtually we'd no business there as it isn't open to visitors. Bill and I found we'd a little wooden cubicle each, complete with camp bed (outrageous luxury for two such hardened old campaigners).

Tea over in Mrs. Eales' cosy kitchen, we went with Ted along the Point towards Cley. By now the rain was beginning, a rain which was to keep on for almost every minute of our stay at Blakeney. It was a bad night for migrants. Had the wind been in the right quarter, north-easterly, the soueda bushes, so Ted told us, would have been alive with them. All we saw was a draggled rabbit and a single, golden-crested wren which must have been newly in.

And this brings me to the migration of the birds, those travellers of the upper skies who, during the autumn nights, come to our shores in their thousands. Blakeney Point, and indeed all this stretch of coast, is the first landfall for the birds making the North Sea crossing from Heligoland. It's a sort of airport and, when the winds are favouring and the night is right, many hundreds of utterly weary and spent birds drop to the shelter of the dunes. Thankful they must be the crossing is over and done, and there they can rest before journeying on. Twelve hours or more they stay and then pass on upon their mysterious travels.

On the western tip of Blakeney Point the terns nest in summer-time. But when I went there at September's end, only a few young ones were on the wing; the main flocks had gone back to Africa. They'll be back at Blakeney next late April and early May as they have been for as long as Norfolk men can remember. Looking at those few I saw that evening flying up the shore against the grey sky and spitting rain, I thought how wonderful it was that in a few days they would be feeling the fierce warmth of the tropics. That those frail, lithesome bodies, those fragile bones, should voyage so far seemed unbelievable! And there, perhaps, you have the answer to those who say "so you're a *bird-watcher!*" in rather puzzled and pitying tones.

That's why we watch the birds, for their beauty, their grace; each species with its differing individual ways and habits, and maybe because of a wistful envy that we also could lift silent wings and roam the skyways of the world!

The driving rain and gathering dark turned us back at last, and as we went I saw upon the sands the remains of a more sinister bird of passage: the gaunt, black shell of the first Heinkel to be shot down on this coast. Its ugly, black nose looks towards its home hive, Germany, an empty, futile wreck, a monument to the folly of mankind. The marshes here are strewn with other wrecks, but they are old, honest wrecks of crab-boats and dredgers, victims of age, wind, and weather. Each has its story, each gives a name to the dunes and ridges hard by. It was the tarred and blackened timbers of the old *Britannia,* an oyster dredger, which lighted up the great fire-place of our cosy quarters that night.

By the leaping tawny flames, Eales told us many a tale of the Point, how one year, for instance, a great sea eagle came and haunted the dunes for many days and how Ted trembled for its safety. For, believe it or not, there are still those blighted minds who wish to slay the rare wild-bird—it's really a form of vicious greed!

I awoke in the early hours and, opening wide the window, I looked out on the night. Before me stretched the whitish dunes. They were clearly visible, for behind the rain-clouds shone a nearly full moon.

There was no wind at all, but the rain fell softly and steadily and somewhere a gutter was running. At times there came over the dunes a hollow, sudden thunder, indeed I thought it was thunder until I realized it must be the rollers just over the ridge. But it struck me as being no ordinary noise of the sea. It was really, now I come to think of it, a truly titanic noise, which began and ceased abruptly like a discharge of ordnance. I remembered a reference to it in a book I found in the students' book-case. It told of the 'roaring' heard on windless nights from the old boat-house. It is an unexplained phenomenon and is locally known as 'the sea crying for the wind'. A nice expression, I think. I imagined the sea as some vast monster out of sight over the shingle bank, stirring in its sleep and giving a sudden agonized moan for a freshening wind.

Next morning the rain still fell and the wind had come (the sea's desire had been gratified). Not far from the boat-house Bill and I lay on a shingle ridge and watched some grey plovers feeding on the sand. What beautiful birds they are: larger than our familiar peewit, or green plover, with a mottled grey back and what looks like a velvety black waistcoat which buttons neatly under the chin like a cravat—a most notable aristocrat which one may sometimes see between the tides on the Norfolk Coast.

With a falling tide and breakfast over, we took the motor-boat, with Ted at the helm, away down channel to see the seals. From afar, as they lie stretched asleep on the sand-bars, lulled by the tumble of the rollers, these strangely pathetic fur-clad people of the sea appear like so many bolsters strewn upon the golden sand. A solitary young one lay asleep on top of a bank and, throttling down, Ted steered straight for it. The seal awoke and came flopping frantically down the sand like a fat baby whose ankles have been tied. The sand spurted sideways from its flippers, in its great round eyes was a terror inherited.

On the land they are ungainly, helpless things, these little fur-clad men and women: once in the water they become swift and lovely beings. As we chugged along the sand-bar, hugging the edge, black knobs peered over with something like horror on each bewhiskered face. There was a muffled noise as the herd went frantically thumping down the sand slopes, and when we turned the corner we were just in time to see the boil of water where they'd dived, not more than twenty yards distant.

The seals, who should by now have come (rightly) to regard men as an enemy of their kind, still wish to be friends with us. Maybe, too, they have an insatiable curiosity and have never learnt that men can strike death from a distance. So lo and behold! in a moment, one round head after another bobbed up, smooth and black like the wet heads of boy bathers. These were mostly young, though I noticed one or two old ones farther out. Was it malignant hatred in those round eyes I saw or a simple wonderment? But soon they had no doubt that we were hostile, for one after another they rode the waves over the bar like leaping black horses, and over beyond they sat back in the white smother as if they were in submarine arm-chairs, staring back at us, bobbing and peering at our boat, which was swinging back against the fast-ebbing tide.

It's a pity that the fishermen on the coast have to shoot the seals. But it must be remembered that they are increasing enormously, and what a big, old dog seal needs in the way of daily fish is nobody's business. Before the war a sum of 10/- was given for each seal's mask, but now I don't think this offer stands. The pelts and oil seem to have little market value.

By the time we'd got back to the hut, it was midday. The rain was increasing and the wind blowing hard. Every gutter was running and we ourselves were wet. Garments had to be dried, so while the rain beat savagely on the windows we got the fire going once more with the tarry timbers of the old *Britannia*, and while our coats and trousers were steaming Ted Eales showed us bird books, records, and old, faded photographs of bygone incidents on the Point.

What a whole history lies in those faded photographs which date back to Edwardian times! Ladies in leg-of-mutton blouses and stiff collars; gentlemen in Alpine hats, long beards, breeches, and gaiters; these early twentieth-century 'gull warriors', both male and female, how earnestly they seek for rare botanical speci-mens, how decorously they sit and picnic there in those far-off spacious summers! And looking at those photographs (records of an instant of forgotten time) one can see how the dunes change shape down the years; some are much higher now, indeed many of the dunes are rising yearly.

In one place on the Point, Eales showed us a vast crater in the sand like a bowl of a volcano, a sand blow. Here the wind, by freakish chance, whirls round and round like a carpenter's 'bit'. Standing at the bottom, one sees nothing but the sky overhead with its scudding clouds and a fringe of marram grass fluttering in the winds.

Behind the old lifeboat-house is a well which supplies the Point. Beautiful fresh water it is, drawn from a bore which is not deeply sunk in the sand. It's within a hundred yards of the sea, which is just over the dunes. Yet there is no brackish taste to this water, nor the slightest trace of salt.

It wasn't until after five that the flowing tide made it possible to embark once more for the shore and home. We left in a final terrific downpour which soaked us through. I had hoped to go on to the bird sanctuary at Cley, but darkness was not far off, the rain was redoubling in fury and, to make matters worse, we couldn't start my car which is temperamental in damp weather.

So Ted had to come to the rescue with his truck and give us a towing start. It was six o'clock before we were finally off, and two hours later found us still battling grimly across the Lincolnshire fens in the teeth of a raging wind and through what seemed like a deluge of Biblical dimensions. To make matters worse, we had a puncture—but I'll draw a veil over these tribulations.

Despite the weather, despite everything, we thoroughly enjoyed our brief stay on Blakeney Point; and if the reader happens to be a bird- or nature-lover and you relish the level marshlands and wide skies, the thin keening of gulls and the distant thunder of white surf—go to Blakeney Point.

7. A Night to Remember

I AM writing this chapter in the quiet of my studio. It is an autumn night, humid and still, and now and again a moth comes in and flies aimlessly round the light.

When I put my dogs to bed in the garage a few minutes ago, before coming up here to the top of the house, I noticed the last remaining swallow, the feeble one of the brood, which roosts on the cross-beam close to its old nest.

This was one of a second brood, and its parents, brothers and sisters started on their long journey three days ago. Soon this little chap will also depart,* and he is wisely gathering strength for that great adventure which he may have to face alone.

Seeing him roosting there reminded me that in another week or so the grey geese will be likewise setting out for these shores. And thinking of the geese leads to other memories.

Something in the utter quiet of this room (with the only sound a far-off intermittent hooting of tawny owls in the woods of the park) turns my mind to those nights spent far out on the lonely tideways when I have had no companion, not even a dog, to keep me company. And there passes before me a succession of pictures. The moonlit sloblands of Fenham Slakes on the Northumberland Coast, the frost sending blue lights from the frozen sea-wrack, the cheeping of little knot, busy at their feed . . . that time when Charles and I lay out on the frozen mud on a night of intense frost. Even the warmth of our bodies failed to soften the frozen

* He left ten days after these notes were written—on the 12th of September.

42

mud beneath us and over all rode a proud, full moon, and all was silence, and stars.

That other night away on a hill pasture, when we waited for the geese to come. Again it was frosty and snow was on the ground; again it was bitter cold, with a full moon.

There have been similar nights on the marshes of the Wash, so silent and still that even the moonbeams seemed frozen.

There is an overwhelming sense of peace at such a time which only those who have experienced it can comprehend. The lust to shoot and kill is present in the background, I suppose. That is the reason why you are there, stretched out under the 'brew' of the merse, staring up at the stars.

Yet you almost forget the wildfowl in the majesty and peace of night and moonlight. Even the little waders seem to be absent, for the tide is barely on the turn and is somewhere far out there across that greenish plain which is the playground of wind and wave.

Though it is a night of frost you do not feel chilled, for your leather, wool-lined jacket defies all wind and weather. It is an air-man's jacket and belonged (so the faded ink letters tell me) to a certain Flight Sergeant Ames, R.A.F. I wonder where he is now and if he survived those dark years of war? Are you there, Flight Sergeant? Perhaps this jacket has been over Berlin with the flak bursting and the groping searchlights swinging. . . . Quite an adventurous jacket. . . .

This question of the right clothing is all-important, especially when you have passed the forties. Youngsters don't seem to mind how they dress for fowling and they suffer extreme discomfort at times. I can't enjoy myself if I'm really cold and it spoils half the fun.

It has been a long tramp over rough ground to reach this hiding-place of mine under the 'brew'. I sweated profusely even though I'd undone the zip of the jacket. When I took off my hat I could see the steam rising from it in the moonlight.

But now the exertion is over and I lie and watch the shining sands in front. The moon is well up, and across the firth I can see a dim loom of high hills. They look near but they must be six miles or more across the bay. Though there is no wind down here, I can see small, fleecy clouds passing over very gently; they must be three or four thousand feet up. Occasionally they drift across the moon. When this happens the greenish light is dimmed, and if you look closely at the sands you can see the cloud shadow travelling slowly along, just like the shadow of a summer cloud along the side of a fell or a meadow.

All this time the ear is straining and the senses are alert. You are not aware of this at first and then, as it were, you suddenly catch yourself listening intently, and find you are subconsciously holding your breath. Very far away, on the edge of hearing, there is a faint crying. It may be a big, black-backed gull, or more likely, a curlew; it is a second or two before you can identify it.

Yes, it *is* a curlew, passing along the fringe of the tide. The sound, for a second or so, is quite distinct and then passes away eastwards over the lonely flats.

If you turn a little under the miniature cliff of turf (you are lying in its shadow), you can see a line of brilliant, jewel-like harbour lights which appear to be dancing up and down like marionettes. Why they dance like this, I do not know. It is understandable with the stars far up there above you in the black holes in the fleecy clouds. And it is strange, too, how the reflections of these man-made stars are drawn out over the gleaming sands to a point almost within gunshot of your hide.

The shining path of the moon's reflection is almost like the illumination from the headlamp of a car. Studying this for minutes on end you can see, now and again, the small, swift form of a wader pass across it, and sometimes, if you are lucky, the black, flogging silhouettes of silent geese.

On such a night as this when all is so still, greylags will often

44

pass quietly along off-shore. They may be aware of others farther down the estuary, and there is plenty of room here, many miles of moonlit ooze. Maybe somewhere down-river there is a favourite sand-bar where the geese rest. They are making for that.

Again there is that hush, like the hush of death. Now can imagination rove. You think of many things, but mostly the mind just drifts and you don't think of anything: a sort of half-sleep and yet you are very much awake, there is no sense of drowsiness.

If you stare up at the slow-moving clouds and at the dark spaces in between, these spaces appear as ragged black holes. And if you look long enough you find you are falling into them and the brain becomes quite dizzy. It is not a very pleasant feeling.

Those sinister ebony lakes remind one of those other black depths we read about far under the sea where no light can penetrate. The only living creatures there have a sponge-like texture because of the enormous pressures; some carry with them mysterious lights to guide them through those dreadful abysses.

The inky darkness of outer space and the deepest seas is to me truly terrifying and does not bear thinking about.

It is more pleasant and restful to let the eyes rove over the shining sands and to enjoy the silence of this magical night. The cold air is spiced with the scent of salt and sea-wrack, mingled with a certain moorland smell. This heathery, piney smell must come from the wooded hills around, but to the keen nose it is only just discoverable. The smell of the sea itself is predominant. Mixed with it there is the sharp accent of frost. A foggy night smells quite differently; so does a night of wind, and storm.

Somehow, when watching this tranquil, moonlit scene, the memories of other nights along this coast cannot be recaptured, nights when the great winds were up and out and there was sleety rain or driving snow.

There is no sense of peace then, all is war, turmoil, and clamour.

The wildfowl hate a night of gales, for they are buffeted unmercifully. One must remember that a big bird like a goose, indeed any bird, must try to keep its head to wind. To have a full nor'easter or a westerly gale blowing up your backside must be acutely uncomfortable. Your tail (even a short one) is blown backwards and every feather turned inside out. Remember, too, that flying into a gale for a big bird like a goose, which has a wing-spread of several feet, must be a most exhausting process. They can't just go with the wind like a sailing-boat, for an off-shore gale will whirl them far out to sea.

But it is no time to talk of strife and noise. This is a calm night of frost and moon, with the tide at the ebb. But we have been sitting here talking like this, and now the tide has turned.

All at once you are aware of it. At first you guessed that faint murmur was a train passing along the opposite shore. Then you realize that it is the oncoming tide. And at once the picture changes. Even a little breeze comes from nowhere and moves the grass on top of the brew. And there are sounds now in plenty, faint as yet but growing. The first you notice is the very musical yodelling of the curlew packs. They are overjoyed at the prospect of food, and as the thin silken film of sea water swills gently over the firm sand, shrimps and other minute sand creatures stir and come to life. They are at it now all down the tide, and mingled with the ceaseless 'courlees' are the shrill pipes of the oyster-catchers. These black and white magpies of the tidal wastes are more excitable than the long-nosed curlews.

They are absurdly gay with their brilliant orange beaks and legs and their vivid black and white attire. Silvery clouds of knot and dunlin, redshanks with them, are now moving hither and thither along the edge of the incoming water.

All this advancing bustle and noise rouses you from your reverie. You sit up and realize for the first time you feel chilled.

The next thing you notice is that what a moment ago was firm sand, out there in front, is now crinkling water which reflects the moon. Ripple on ripple come washing in sideways and across, breaking with a gentle swilling hiss and minute bubbles.

Every shallow pan and gutter of the sands is filling and brimming. It's amazing how stealthily the tide creeps in, cutting in behind you if you are out from the land, brimming, flooding, and spilling over to continue that onward glide. And after this first filmy skin of water which comes washing in over the flat sands there follows the tide proper, a miniature Severn Bore it seems, sizeable waves curving and breaking in one continuous, murmuring roar.

I could watch for ever the coming of the tide on a quiet winter's night of moon and stars. It is a scene which must be dear to the heart of every wildfowler.

Soon there is water sucking and gulping obscenely among the hollows of the 'brew'. It comes washing in round your waders and retreats again, gathering itself for another onslaught.

And everywhere are birds, birds—the night is full of wings and cryings. Curlews, redshanks, dunlins, 'oysters'—they are all in the air at once. It is amazing where they have all come from. The answer, of course, is that they were out on the tide edge and have retreated before it to the shore.

And then comes the moment you have been waiting for. Above the bustle and roar of the breaking tide, above the yodelling and the pipes, the reedy cheeps, and harsh alarm notes of the 'shank, there comes the yelping of the barnacle geese.

I do not think that the cackling of greylags or the chorus of the pinks is quite so moving as the sound of a barnacle pack in full cry. It is unearthly. Phantom hounds most certainly and Herne the Hunter should be riding after!

Wildly you look to left, to right: to the moon's path now rocking and tossing: to the dark solemn edge of the brew. You cannot tell where they are coming or if, indeed, they will come at all.

And then for a fleeting moment you see them, or rather half-see them. They pass, not along the tide edge where you expected them to pass, but well inshore behind you, not five feet above the close-cropped merse, a moving, nebulous cloud, dim and speeding. Had you been forty yards back from the brew in that gulley you jumped over on your way out, you would have had the whole pack over you!

A moment—and they have gone, and the ear follows them as they pass along the lonely marshes away to the river's mouth.

For you the spell is broken. This land of the Sleeping Beauty is no more, you somehow feel this is the end of the act. Your gun-barrels may be as clean as when you got out of the car and no warm bulge is felt in the goose-bag which hangs on your left hip.

But that does not matter, not one little bit. If you are a true fowler and lover of that magic land 'between the tides', it has been a night to remember.

8. The Mill o' Monteagle

THOSE sky gypsies, the pinkfeet, are a restless tribe, even in a land where they have found secure pasturage. They may feed for a few days (usually three or four) on some chosen field and nobody molests them. But a change of weather, perhaps, or simply a love of wandering and exploration, makes them go elsewhere to seek fresh fields.

One morning the tide may be musical with their battalions and the watcher in the dyke sees the long, weaving skeins go in, the next dawn the estuary is vacant and silent save for a few greylags and the resident wader flocks.

These wanderings may take them to another seaboard, the Wash, the Severn, or some lonely loch among the hills where man seldom goes. I believe they have certain remote Highland lochs to which they repair when they need a complete rest—possibly when they have been much harried by gunners—though they can never long be absent from the salty muds and the sound and movement of the tideways.

At times they still use the estuary as a dormitory, but change their pasturage ashore, coming back to the sea once in the twenty-four hours for salt and grit and a smell of the sea, without which they cannot live.

These secret feeding grounds may be in the most unlooked-for places, and it takes a good deal of scouting and inquiry from the 'locals' to find where the birds are going.

This was so during one winter just after the war when the old gang—David, myself and my cousin Tony—were working

49

one of the northern firths. An account of this may be of interest.

When we arrived, there were a lot of pinks on the bay and they were using a stubble about four miles from the shore. According to the locals they had been coming to this field at night for over a week and we hoped for great things. We built hides in the dyke bordering the stubble and went next evening (it was almost the full-moon period) but not a goose showed up. All we shot was a mallard which fell to David.

But as the moon rose we heard some big lots passing in on our right, heading for the mountains. The following morning we went to the shore and saw the pinks come back in force. That evening they again made away to the northwards over the mountains. They had evidently found fresh pasturage. It was up to us to find exactly where.

David spread out the map on the table of our fowling H.Q. and together we tried to locate the most likely spots.

Beyond that mountain range were several lochs, some of considerable size and some set far from any road. Any of these might be their goal, though I had the idea that they were using some stubble in the wide strath of arable land which lay on the far side of the range.

The moon was nearly full and the geese would be feeding at night, and I argued that the lochs were not the attraction: it was food they were after. At the period of the full moon, night is the most favoured time for feeding. One must remember that they are large birds and need a considerable amount of food to keep them going. A large gaggle of pinkfeet will eat as much as a small flock of sheep. Actually they are beneficial to grass pasture as they manure the ground, and the farmers do not mind them. It is only when they start on springing crops that the damage is done, but this does not occur until the end of the winter.

David pointed with his pencil-stub to a narrow road which

wound away through a pass in the mountains some six miles to the east of where the geese went over that morning.

"That's our road; let's go and see. We'll have a look at the loch nearest the road; the others we can't explore; but we'll just hope they aren't there."

Soon after breakfast we climbed into the shooting-brake and were soon on our way, steadily climbing the winding road which led to the top of the pass. There was a mild mist over the river valley behind us, but as we climbed the air became so cold we had to shut the windows and set the defroster going.

There was ice on the road too, and soon—snow. It was amazing how quickly scenery and mood seemed to change. We left behind the warm fir woods with their red-bracken floors and glimpses of tumbling burns, and soon there were no trees, nothing but barren, high tops of rich-toned heather patched with frozen snow. The road was treacherous too, and now and again we felt the stern of the van slide and wag.

At last we reached the top and, pulling in to the side of the track, we got out of the van with the spy-glass. On all sides the heather stretched away. On our right was a yet higher ridge, topped by a small, thick wood of hardy firs which stood out boldly against the skyline. Below us on the left the ground fell away into the misty strath shrouded in wintry vapour.

Somewhere in this direction the geese must have their pasturage, but whether this was near the lochs we had seen on the map or on the flat lands, how could we know? We might be within a couple of miles of their ground or might well be a dozen miles or more distant. The only point in our favour was that a gaggle of two hundred or so pinkfeet are not easily concealed, especially if they are feeding on the arables, and inspection of the stubbles would give us a clue.

Of course, should they be on the remote lochs we had seen on the map, that was another matter; there was no way of getting at them save by interception on the shore. Even in the Highlands you can't go 'brassing about' wherever you like. Some of the remote lochs are well keepered by local lairds who are not so easily persuaded as the farmers.

Scotch farmers are a truly grand race, and very rarely have I been refused permission to try for geese. It is the cad who pretends he is after geese when he is in reality out for a full day's shooting at anything he can see which spoils the game for honest fowlers. I have often been told by Highland farmers I may shoot grouse, pheasants, and partridges, when after geese, but I never do so. Even a grouse is scorned if geese are in the offing.

After scanning the ridge on both sides, we went on down towards the strath. Then a bend in the road revealed an old grey-stone building set in the hollow of a burn. Very old sycamore-trees crowded it in and a lively little burn chattered merrily under a disused and crumbling mill-wheel. Close by, too, there were the remains of the mill-pond, choked now with willow and coarse rush. On our map this building was marked 'Mill of Monteagle'.

We found the farmer busy in his yard loading manure which steamed in the frosty air. Here was a useful man who, living on the spot, might have some news of the grey legions which we had seen these last few days heading in this direction.

"Aie, aie, the geese" (Scotchmen pronounce 'geese' in quite a different way from the Sassenach but it cannot be spelt, it is just the way they say it), "the geese are aboot and were over here the nicht. They'll be using the top stubble. I pute them off there yesterday morning . . . aie."

He raised his finger and pointed to the ragged firs on the skyline. "Yon's the field, on the ither side of yon firs. It's a barley stubble and the ducks are worrkin' it at nicht too. Aie, ye can have a goo at the geese . . . Sairtenly! Sairtenly!"

His daughter, a fine buxom girl, was helping him load the manure, and we could not help wondering what chances she had of a gay time in that remote spot. The Mill o'Monteagle might be entrancing enough to the nature-lover and sportsman, but hardly the sort of place where an attractive, full-blooded young lassie would find all that was her due.

These Highland water-mills lack the homely, sleepy air of our own water-mills of the south. I always associate the latter with high June, flies weaving over the pond, the faintly-heard hiss of the mill-leat among willows, and that fruity exciting aroma of swamp and river water, and of course the lusty fish which cruise around the mossy piles.

These Highland mills are grey and weather-beaten, crouching under the lee of the hills and with boulders in place of reed beds. It must have been many a long year since the broken wheel revolved in the current of the tumbling burn, large now with the winter rains, rushing and roaring among its stones. There was frozen snow a little way up the hill-side and icicles hung from the mill-wheel like a castle's portcullis.

Thanking the farmer, we went back up the track a little way and following his directions left the van in a gateway. Then we set off to climb the hill. Here and there we ploughed through snow and our feet sank in the heather. We put up some grouse near the skyline and a curlew rose from the heather to go crying over the misty valley.

It took us almost an hour to reach the stone wall below the fir wood beyond which was the stubble, and by that time the afternoon was beginning to grey. From our vantage point we could see right away to the firth, which shone faintly in the wintry evening light to the south.

As our sole mission was to scout the ground, we had not prepared to stay. In any case, a moonlight foray needs a little preparation in the matter of a well-filled flask of rum and so forth. But if we could find abundant goose 'sign', it would be worth our while to come on the following night.

We clambered over the wall and soon gained the fir wood. There was a lot of snow up there, but on the bare stubble beyond, the wind had blown it fairly bare on the ridges.

It was a largish field, so we separated. I took the north side, David the centre, and Tony the south section. It was not long before we found abundant evidence of midnight visitations. There was goose 'sign' everywhere, and the snow-powdered stubbles were criss-crossed with a maze of large webbed footprints. Geese had evidently been using the field for a considerable time, for my experienced eye noted much old goose sign as well as fresh. Here and there a bird had sat down and had a nap. There was the hollow in the snow made by its breast and a little pile of droppings at one end.

All three of us made the same report, that there was most 'sign' at the south end near the stone wall.

By the time we got back to the car it was almost dark and an owl was hooting in the fir wood. It must have made him a draughty bedroom.

That night, when David went out of our fowling quarters to rug up the van (it had to be parked in the open inn yard), he came back with the report that thick cloud was coming up from the north and it was beginning to snow. Any secret schemes we had for going back to the field that same night were accordingly squashed, and we only hoped the fall would not be too heavy to make the passage of the hills impossible on the following evening.

Next morning dawned clear and frosty, and there had been only a light fall which would not be enough to stop us, at least so we hoped, though it was difficult to judge what depth had fallen on the high ground.

At about four o'clock that afternoon, we set out again fully prepared to stay out the night on the hill. As we began the long climb to the pass, we looked back to see a huge, rose-red sun going down over the firth. Flocks of pigeons were going to roost in the thick fir woods of Fusshie Priory.

As we gained altitude, the snow became deeper. I began to doubt whether we should get the van on to the high ground by the Mill o'Monteagle, but we did, after getting stuck twice on the frozen road, a contingency we had provided for with spade and chains.

The van was parked in the gateway and well rugged up, and we set òff once more to climb to the wood. This was more ex-hausting than on the previous day, but we at last reached the top and rested in the shadow of the firs.

A lot of pigeons went out as we reached the trees and, as we did not expect the geese until the moon rose, we had twenty minutes' good shooting at them as they came back. When the flight was over we went out on the stubble after drawing for places. David was the centre gun, Tony was to the south, and I was to the north, choosing a spot where the goose droppings were thick.

I spread out my lying-sheet and, making my labrador sit close beside me, I settled down to wait. All over the field there were relatively bare places which had been cleared of snow by the wind, so that we had a tolerable background. To ambush geese on virgin snow without a white covering is inadvisable on a moon-light night; the dark form of a man can be very conspicuous. Luckily there was no wind on this high field, or it would have made our long wait an uncomfortable one, despite the fact we were warmly clad. Even so, the old dog was shivering and was glad to creep close beside me.

For a long time after sunset I could see the dark form of David very clearly as he sat in the centre of the field about a hundred and fifty yards to my right, and beyond him the fainter darker smudge of Tony. But gradually, as the light faded, those dim forms melted into their background and soon the only visible thing was the black mass of the fir wood showing over the white rim of the hill.

From my high vantage point I could just see a single, bright light from the Mill o'Monteagle down in the glen, where the farmer and his family were cosily sitting down to supper (no doubt listening to the 6 o'clock news on the wireless).

The stars shone frostily high above and I heard the owl hooting in the firs. He had had a noisy awakening when we were shooting at the pigeons (we had bagged seven birds) and I hoped that he was also in for a noisy night as well!

Before the moon rose I heard mallard quacking and once or twice the wicker of wings and glimpsed a dark shape passing swiftly over with that peculiar thin whistling. We had arranged not to fire at anything but geese, or I should have had a smack at them. One duck actually pitched on the snow within thirty yards of me but immediately sprang up again and was lost against the stars.

The cold clamped down with great ferocity. It came as stealthily as the tide, worming its way inside my clothing, and Judy cuddled ever closer, grumbling a little under her breath. Now and again waves of shuddering passed through her (and me, as she was pressed tightly up against my side), but I suspect it was excitement as much as a sense of chill.

Just as the moon rose out of the misty vapour I heard the distant yelp of a single pinkfoot to the north, but saw nothing. Half an hour passed without any other promise.

Waiting for geese is rather like waiting for a coarse fish to bite. You are full of eagerness at first and sit as still as a rock watching, hoping, and waiting. And then one's enthusiasm begins to ebb away and your feet begin to tingle. The cold of the gun-barrels in the crook of my arm was felt through my leather sleeve and the moonlight began to glisten on the small corn-stalks which showed above the snow. I felt horribly conspicuous, and now I could see

David again quite clearly, and even Tony beyond him. There was a defined shadow now on the snow behind me.

Something came over the white rim of the hill on my left, a cautious, halting spectre. I thought at first it was a fox setting out for his night's hunting, but soon saw it was a hare. It passed across between David and myself and vanished in the direction of the fir wood.

I was just on the point of rising to my feet and having a 'cab-man's' warm as my finger tips had no feeling in them, when I dis-tinctly heard the sound of geese approaching from my left. This was rather unexpected as I thought they would be sure to come in from the firth and so over Tony and David.

By the sound, it was a big skein and as the seconds passed the babel of cries came ever nearer, which was exciting. They were evidently circling the field, for the next moment I heard them over the fir wood, swinging round. Were they going to lower or had they seen us in the moonlight and were passing on to the lower lands of the strath?

I pivoted round, staring into the greenish, moonlit sky, my eyes full of stars. The crying loudened, and a moment later I heard Tony fire both barrels. There was a moment's silence as the geese climbed, and then they came baying right over my head. I could see them fairly well. I stood up and fired both barrels at one bird which was directly overhead outlined against the thin, fleecy cloud. Immediately it seemed to swell in size and, with a whistling rush, hit the snow with a tremendous thump not ten yards behind me. Judy went out and brought it back.

After that there was a pause of about ten minutes. I called out to David to know whether Tony had a bird down but received no reply, so concluded he hadn't heard me. Then I saw a dim figure walking about at the far end of the field, so I imagined Tony was gathering his goose. I hoped so, anyway, for I had heard no thump after his shot.

Then I heard the geese again, this time coming in from the firth. They circled as before, but they were high and none of us (very wisely) attempted to fire, though they came over us in a gliding, scattered mass. They all alighted at the far end of the field and remained quite silent, so much so that I thought they must have gone. But on peering into the half-darkness I thought I could see a black shadow on the snow. They must have been about 100 yards from me and were probably a little nearer to David. Anyway, it was wise to let them stay, for others were coming and those on the field would act as decoys.

This lot, a party of thirty or more 'pinks', came sailing in with paddles down almost on top of David. I heard him fire twice and also heard at least one goose hit the snow. The next moment they all came over me in a frantic hurry and climbing. I had an easy one on my right and hit a second bird which fell slanting, some way off on the edge of the stubble. I was afraid it was a runner and might get into the heather, so I sent the dog for it and she brought it back in about seven minutes.

After this episode there was a long lull during which time we all got up and stretched our legs and tried to get some warmth back into our limbs by pulls at the flask. Tony had had a goose, and David two, which made our bag six, and still another four or five hours to go to daylight, so we weren't doing too badly.

Soon after midnight a very large skein came in. David missed with both shots. I also distinguished myself by missing, un-accountably, as they came past me on my left within thirty yards. Perhaps they were farther than they seemed, but we should have had one, if not two, out of this lot.

This concluded our night's foray at the Mill o'Monteagle, for though we waited another two killing hours on that frozen hill-top, no other geese were heard or seen, and it was three very cold and weary men who stumbled down the snow-clad hill to the warmth of the waiting van. But our bag of six geese was ample reward for frozen hands and toes, and it will be a long while before any of us forget that wonderful moonlight vigil at the Mill o'Monteagle.

We have since visited the locality many times both by day and night, but have never again found the geese there. Alas! they do not come to that district in the numbers they did, and the reason is, I think, that the building of an R.A.F. station in the vicinity has scared them away.*

* The R.A.F. station is now derelict, but the geese still haven't returned

9. Hey! Ho! The Wind and the Rain

THAT'S the answer to the fowler's prayer—wind and rain, but especially wind. A driving rain is perhaps the most uncomfortable of all the bad weather the fowler has to face, and it calls for more endurance than snow or frost.

I don't mind walking in a 'head' rain, I relish riding on horseback with the rain smacking against my teeth, but I don't like sitting motionless in a downpour. Ugh!

I'm thinking of the time when I wore a cap for fowling. Now a cap is all right in moderate weather but when it gets sodden and starts to dribble, then it's worse than useless. It, of course, dribbles as merrily as any gutterspout from the *peak*, but that falls clear of your face. It is the flank attack that matters, the time the actual body of the cap gets wet and starts to 'bleed'. No neckwear is proof against a trickle down the short hairs.

But wear a deerstalker and the water is shed clear all round your face, in fact in heavy rain it's rather entertaining, that ring of pearl-like drops which forms a fringe to your immediate horizon —it's almost a decoration!

There's one drawback. Being waterproof, they are not easily

cleaned, at least, I have always found that when they come back from the cleaners they are half their former size.

A waterproof hat, being non-porous, cannot allow the head to sweat as it should and, believe me, when you have a lot of bog-tramping to do, even on the coldest day, you perspire a good deal, especially about the head. The hat in time becomes impregnated with stale sweat (you must excuse these unsavoury details but they are important) and before you have had your deerstalker a year your fellow guns will look at you askance with that 'even his best friend wouldn't tell him' expression. And that is, I find, the only draw-back to a deerstalker. It's a pity because the genuine article is not easy to get. I'm not talking about the round tweed hats favoured by North Country shepherds and farmers, but the hat which is slightly peaked fore and aft, not with an exaggerated peak such as is seen in the old drawings of our friend Sherlock Holmes, but a modest South-African War era kind of peak.

There's one other drawback—they are very expensive (when you can get them).

The whole secret of watertight clothing is to have your garments with a good overlap, like a well-slated roof. Remember water runs downwards (though on a rough, wild morning on the coast it seems to come at you from all points of the compass and defies the law of gravitation).

Satisfactory covering for the hands is not so easy. You need a pliable trigger finger. Mittens are the best in dry weather, but in rain or snow they are useless. Leather gloves are the best, wool-lined, with the trigger finger cut off. And your jacket sleeves should come *over the edge of the gloves* so as to shed the water clear. If your sleeves are short, the rain runs off the cuff *into* your gloves.

The same care must be taken to see that the shooting coat is not too short. The lower edge should come well over your thigh wader tops. Thigh waders, though heavy to walk in, are essential, even on a 'short' marsh, for there is always the possibility of a stalk.

It is perfectly sensible to take these measures which ensure that you keep dry and warm in the wettest weather. You will enjoy yourself much more, for there is nothing so miserable as wet clothes: they are worse than water in your waders, which soon heats up to the body temperature if you are walking about.

A wild and windy morning on the coast is exhilarating and always exciting. Fowl will most surely be on the wing. I have a note of one such morning when there was almost a full S.W. gale which made even the comparatively short walk to the sea wall an exhausting business. We had heard the wind in the night knocking at the windows of our H.Q. and now and again a rattle of sleet hitting the glass as though someone had hurled a handful of gravel at the panes.

But when we went out just after 6 a.m., the night was fine, though the wind was blowing with force, roaring in the tall beech-trees round the inn. By the time I had chosen my hide on the marshes, the dawn was coming up, and, as the light grew, an impressive array of huge inky clouds, wild in the extreme, came rapidly over the hills, crossing the glow in the eastern sky. It was quite fascinating to watch these masses of vapour careering across the dawn glow with tremendous speed, mighty cloud ships in full sail. The tide, which was coming in, made a great roaring. From my hiding-place I could see white horses rising and falling out in the firth. As for the geese, they were visible and sometimes audible (in snatches) as soon as there was any light in the sky.

They were unable to rest on the sand-banks or the sea and they began going in very early with the wind in their tails. What was most surprising to me was the number of mallard and wigeon. Usually at morning flight I saw a few small parties of duck, but on this particular morning we must have seen hundreds and all were coming off the land in the teeth of the wind, flying very low, barely head high. Once ducks are on water, wind does not seem to worry them as it does geese, possibly because they sit lower and even find some shelter from the waves themselves.

But geese cannot abide sitting out a gale, nor do they like feeding ashore in a high wind. They seem to spend their time making short flights either along the shore or to and from the land. On such a day of wind, you can have a chance of shore shots from flight time to flight time.

These ducks, mostly mallard, which I saw toiling in over the marshes offered some splendid opportunities, and though geese were everywhere that morning, we could not resist shooting at the mallard too. We had eight in the bag and lost three more which the dogs could not find. All this before the really big 'pink' skeins came in off the sea. We made bad shooting at the latter, due no doubt to the speed at which they were travelling. We only had two down from three guns when we should have had four times that figure.

The sound of a high wind roaring in the tree tops and rattling windows is a cheering sound to the fowler's ear. Lying snugly in bed on a moonless night when of course shooting is out of the question, the mind gets busy with one's favourite ambushes down on the firth. You speculate where the best places will be tomorrow at dawn. You must allow for the power and push of the wind, and if you can locate the geese by sound in the darkness, and if you know the firth well, you can get some idea of where they are likely to cross the shore, and so you plan accordingly.

And then, having decided in your mind where you are going, you turn to thinking of the geese themselves. Where are they on such a night?

Somewhere out there in the bellowing darkness, with the waves crashing in a dim white smother along the edge of the brew, those gallant birds must be. On some firths and estuaries there are reeds which give shelter, but on places like the Solway, which I have in mind, there is no such cover save, in places, scrubby gorse bushes which grow on the merse itself. Into the lee of these the geese will often come in the darkness of night, as witnessed by the droppings seen next morning, but it must be a perilous dormitory in a country where foxes abound. A wild goose is never happy when he is ashore and no blame to him! Six pounds or more of succulent goose is a prize for any predatory animal, man included. No wonder the poor birds distrust the land!

Yet to the land they must go for food, unlike the little black brent geese which find their living between the tides, feeding on the zos grass. A brent has no need to cross the high-sea mark, and his only enemy is the puntsman. Brent will occasionally feed on saltings, and I have a record of these geese seen feeding on the fine grass of a golf-course on the coast. But it is a true bird of the slob-lands and maybe more used to buffetings by the sea than the pinks and greys which do not seem ever to leave the more sheltered waters.

In driving snow and sleet all wildfowl are restless and low-flying, offering chances which you may not have at any other time. Never forget that the worst weather for goose hunting is a long frost with snow on the ground; still, hard weather which fastens the stubbles and pastures under lock and key. Even the ducks will leave a firth at such times, and the only birds you will see are the tide-line waders (and even these are less abundant) and a few pricked geese. These poor creatures, unable to fly strongly, have to get along as best as they can by coming in at dusk on the tide and creeping up the gutters on the flow, where they may be able to pluck a few blades of frozen marsh grass.

10. *Straight Shooting*

THE ideal gun for the fowler varies according to the choice of individuals. I have met some men who would never dream of using anything but an ordinary twelve-bore, and I think I should be right in saying that 60 per cent of people who go out after geese and duck do not use anything but this weapon.

I have even met habitual goose-shooters who say they would not use a bigger gun, but when I have talked to them I have found that they have the shooting of preserved ground where the geese are abundant and seldom shot. In these instances geese are nearly always more easy to bag and I would possibly use a similar gun under those conditions.

The lighter the gun the better will you shoot. If I could always use my ordinary game-gun on geese I would do so. But how many of us have the shooting of preserved goose grounds? Possibly under thirty in the whole of Britain! I do not, of course, know what King George VI, an expert shot, used on his Norfolk marshes, but I doubt if he used anything larger than a full-choked twelve-bore. I should be most surprised if he used an eight-bore, but I may be wrong. As everyone knows, His Majesty, in addition to being a first-rate shot, was very keen on wildfowling, and I understand it was his favourite sport. This, if I may say so without disrespect, shows what a discerning sportsman he was.

But to the usual run of fowlers who have to take their sport on the coast, where geese are wild and high, then something more than an ordinary gun is necessary. You would not go out salmon-fishing with a trout rod and trout tackle. Salmon *have* been landed on such gear, indeed I have seen a large salmon caught on a trout fly in Ireland (and successfully brought to bank), but stronger, heavier stuff is necessary if you wish to catch a salmon. The same applies to geese. It is senseless shooting at geese with an ordinary 12 and possible 5 or 6 shot when they are coming in high over the sea-wall. You may hit them if you are a good shot, but you will not drop them. Many will go away to die lingering deaths. The number of geese I have shot which, on examination, had 5 and 6 shot embedded in their paddles is amazing.

On a heavily-shot coast where many local gunners are always out lining the sea-wall (as at Wells in Norfolk), I would consider a full-choked eight-bore the only gun for the job. These great guns will throw a big pattern of large shot with devastating effect, but they have grave drawbacks. For one thing, you should be a heavily-built man to wield a double eight, which may be more than double the weight of a twelve-bore. However big you are, such guns are not easy to swing; on a long tramp over rough ground they are killing things to lug around.

As I have already stated elsewhere, I used to shoot with a single eight for many years and at times did great slaughter with it. But the lack of the second barrel is a grave drawback. How many of of us have missed with the first shot and killed with the second, not only with an eight but a game-gun too?

In fact I would say that the average shot kills more with the second barrel than the first. Many times with my single eight I have had a skein over me in easy eight-bore range. Bang! goes my first shot, and then I stand helpless whilst above me the skein 'towers', offering a glorious chance!

I know I have said all this before, but I must remember that my reader may have been remiss in not having read any of my other books dealing with wildfowl and he is reading about goose-shooting for the first time. So I ask the pardon of the old campaigners who know all the answers and will be thinking that what I am writing is simply padding!

No, I advise you to put away all ideas of using your game-gun on geese and to purchase a three-inch, twelve-bore, either new if you are affluent (and you need to be these days to pay the price), or second-hand if you have modest means. This is without doubt the best possible gun for geese and general wildfowling. You can if you wish use the ordinary short-case cartridge in your Magnum (as the three-inch case gun is called) without damaging the three-inch chambers, though habitual use of short cases in a long-case gun is not recommended.

There are one or two gun firms today who specialize in Magnums, one London firm and a Birmingham firm in particular—no names, no pack drill.

The ammunition is not difficult to get, though it is of course expensive compared to ordinary 2½ cases, but nothing compared to the cost of the vast shells required for the eight-bore. Then goose-shooting does become an expensive business.

For a top-grade, new Magnum of plain design and of sterling quality you will have to pay £80–£90. For a sound, second-hand weapon £45–£50. A stiff price, but if you look after it, it will last indefinitely.*

Now as to ammunition. Again a great controversy always rages on the best shot for geese. A professional fowler I once knew in Scotland used number 3 shot and never anything else. This was on a well-shot coast and he was a crack marksman. Number 3 is certainly a useful size and the pattern is good. In a three-inch case (gun proved for 1½ oz. shot) you have 220 pellets, which should give a useful pattern, this compared to 115 pellets from a three-inch case loaded with BB.

Believe me, those extra pellets are needed when you are out after

* Those were the prices in the early 'fifties! For a good quality foreign Magnum, you will now have to pay £800–£900, and for a top-grade British design £4000–£5000

geese. Of course BB being a much heavier shot has a greater penetration, though the pattern is smaller. At the same time, if you are a really good shot, BB is the size to use. A wild goose needs a terrific blow to bring him to the ground.

My favourite load is BB in the left barrel and 2 in the right, both barrels full-choked.

I have known some fowlers who use SSG for very long shots, and I have myself killed geese at 90–100 yards with this, but it is always a fluke if you bring this off. You get so few pellets to the load and the pattern is non-existent. High shots at geese should never be taken. It is wise to remember that the maximum range of a Magnum is about sixty yards, and the ordinary game-gun will come a long way behind this.

A goose, coming in on an average morning, is usually well above sixty yards away, though he may look a good deal nearer, and even the most experienced fowler will misjudge the height and range. If they are flying parallel to you over water with no background but sea or mud flats, the chances are that they will be 100 yards away when they look 50. If you do not believe me, next time you are on the muds, pace out 50 yards and mark the range. Go back to your former position and the marker will appear in easy distance, a mere 25 yards.

This optical delusion is also noticeable when you see small waders like 'shank and dunlin on the muds when there is no guide in the shape of reeds or stones to give comparison. They appear very much larger than they really are—as big as pigeons.

Length of barrels is another controversial topic. At one time long barrels were the fashion, but it has been proved that a 25-inch barrel will kill almost as well as a 32-inch. But the longer barrel, say a 28-inch, which is the standard length for a Magnum, is useful when you come to use high-velocity cartridges, though even when using the latter you will not gain more than four yards maximum (fluke shots excluded). But if four extra yards do not sound much for a lethal range, I can assure you there are times when those extra feet make all the difference, and certainly in wild-fowling you need a gun that will kill at the greatest possible range and yet not be too heavy to carry.

As to weight of shot, it is interesting to know that BB and 4 shot remain lethal at 60 yards and number 6 shot at 55 yards. But we must remember that firing at, say, a teal at that range, the pattern, being greater, will be more likely to hit a vital spot. One cannot compare the bulk of a goose's body with that of a teal. Though number 4 may kill the teal outright, the goose, even if struck in a vital area, may go on. The heavier shot, 3 2, 1, or the BB's, will have more penetrating power, for the heavier the shot the more the penetration at a given range under 60 yards.

I consider that 3 is too small, and that in my experience BB and numbers 1 and 2 are the best possible sizes for the average shot to use, and I count myself an average shot.*

As to judging ranges, this comes by experience. If hitherto all your shooting has been done inland you will be literally at sea when it comes to shooting on the coastal marshes.

I make it a rule that if I can clearly see the eye of a goose with the pale ring round it, then the bird is a possible shot. If you can't see his eye then he's out of range. Geese overhead are just as hard to judge. They are very big birds. If you could see a partridge flying alongside the average skein which comes in at dawn flight, you would not dream of shooting. Yet time and again, indeed I would say it is the general rule, when the skeins come directly over you, then the impulse to fire is difficult to restrain, even by an experienced fowler.

The paddles should be clearly seen tucked under the tail, and the best possible guide is the swish of their wings. If this is loud, then they are in range; if a mere whisper, then they are not. This, of course, is only applicable to a calm morning and, in

*I now use 3 shot in my right barrel and BB in the left

any case, when there is no wind, the birds will invariably be well up.

Needless to say, sea-water damages a gun dreadfully. Stringent oiling and cleaning is necessary after every trip to the coast. Even a long day on the marshes on a day of gales and rain may damage a gun, and therefore you should have no fancy engraving upon it; it should be as plain as possible.

Personally I prefer a pistol grip to a straight hand stock, but that is a matter of taste. I always think the pistol grip, apart from giving a more comfortable hold, is useful when it comes to carrying the gun under your arm as it lodges easily on the forearm.

I have written many times about gear and clothing for fowling and do not intend to enlarge on these most important items. I would urge, however, the would-be fowler to obtain a really large game-bag, big enough to hold a couple of greylags, one that will serve as a 'sit' bag in a dyke. A damp 'behind' is horrid.

It is amazing how you can fold up a large bird like a wild goose and pack it into a small space. The head should be tucked under the wing—left or right, it does not matter—and the flight feathers held closely to the paddles. The large size 'keepers' game-bag will take two seven-pound 'greys' comfortably.

To carry geese by the paddles is a tedious business. They swing about, the bills knock on the ground and wayward breezes get under the wings.

As to the wild goose's flavour on the table, I find it varies tremendously. Old birds can be very tough even when well hung, and every goose should be hung for a minimum of three weeks before eating. I know some fowlers who would not dream of eating their birds under a month, and even in one case—five weeks. The Irish are said to bury their geese for a month in the ground before eating them. A goose left that long had better be left in peace.

Slow roasting and frequent basting are essential, and it should be roasted with a slice of fat bacon tied round the breast. It should, of course, be stuffed with sage and onions.

Major Pollard, an expert on cookery, has nothing good to say of wild geese on the table. I think his experiments must have been limited and that he was unlucky. Some pinkfeet, especially greys (young birds which have been feeding on stubble), far surpass the domestic goose in flavour and tenderness. They are more 'gamey' and nicer to the palate in every way.

One last word about the actual shooting of geese, and this applies to any game, whether running or flying.

Put out of your mind any question of estimating forward allowance and lead in the terms of mathematics. Tables of forward allowances have been published and mathematically they are correct. For instance, we know that firing with a standard cartridge from a twelve-bore at a bird (not specified!) crossing at 60 yards at 40 m.p.h., a forward allowance of 15 feet should be made. But don't take any notice of these figures. Obey your own instincts and remember above all the cardinal rule that the gun should be swinging as you press the trigger. More geese are missed behind than in front when passing overhead and, in a lesser degree, the same applies to crossing birds, but more often you are below them.

One's instinct is to stop the gun at the moment of pulling the trigger. I only know one gun who was ever able consistently to kill his birds in this way. He made it a rule never to swing, but fired at the place he judged the bird would be when he pressed the trigger.

This is what every beginner does when he starts to shoot, and the result is nearly always a miss. A steady swing, well-balanced feet (no easy matter when in a gutter), and a standing posture are essential to success. Nobody can shoot well when sitting down, and the fowler will do well to remember this. You must certainly keep as low as you can when birds are beating up for your hide, but rise to your feet when you fire. If you do this quietly and smoothly at the critical moment (and that, let me say, calls for nice judgement), the birds may not see you at all. That fat greylag, plummeting from the dawn sky, will have never guessed what hit him.

11. *Stalking and Driving*

THERE are five ways of coming to terms with geese, and for the benefit of the amateur I intend to discuss them here. Old hands can skip this chapter, for I shall be covering familiar ground.

These five ways are as follows:

1. *Ambush:* The creek or hide on the marshes where you intercept the wildfowl on their flights.
2. *Decoying:* Stuffed or imitation geese set up on the feeding grounds with an ambush built within range.
3. *Punting:* Use of a gunning-punt on the open water.
4. *Driving:* Driving feeding geese over an ambush.
5. *Stalking:* Perhaps the most difficult form of getting within range.

We will take these various methods in the order in which they appear, though I say at once, with regard to number 3, I am not well acquainted with this exciting and arduous sport and can only give the views of a landlubber.

First and foremost our aim with a shot-gun is to get within, let us say, a maximum of 60 yards of the wary fowl, if we assume that to be the limit of lethal range. Now over many generations, at least since the invention of the shot-gun, geese have come to know the safe distance, the area, if you like, where they are above ' flak' and beyond fire over 'open sights'. You can kill a goose at 200, 300 yards even, with a rifle, but that, as I have said, is shameful and unsportsmanlike. I can honestly say I have never shot at a goose with a rifle, though I have met so-called sportsmen on the sea-wall armed with ·22's and even ·303's!

That then is our aim, to get within a certain killing range. The ambush is the most usual way and the most profitable. The sitting hide or, when you can get it, the 'standing' hide is the best. You must wear inconspicuous clothing, you must keep absolutely still until the geese are in range, and, wherever possible, the actual shot should be taken *standing up*.

On most marshes there are winding gutters or gullies which serve as natural trenches. Near the sea-wall these are sometimes deep enough to allow you to stand up, but as they wind their tortuous way out to the muds they become wider and shallower, which is a distinct advantage for the quarry we pursue and a dis-advantage to you. For as the geese leave the muds at break of day, they are often just within gun-shot range of the tide edge, but by the time they are over the bank they are high out of shot, in other words, outside the flak area.

I am told that the geese on the Wash are now very seldom within range of the sea-wall. I cannot verify this, for I have not visited the Wash for many years. But when I first shot there this was most certainly not the case, and I have had many a goose from ambushes well in towards the sea-wall and sometimes even from the sea-wall itself. But that was in the days when I was the only gunner for miles of marsh, and now those days have gone for ever.

In shooting geese from marsh ambushes, I would advise the gunner to get as far as he possibly can out towards the fringe of the marsh and choose a narrow gully which, when he sits down, comes up to his chest. This should not be difficult on most coast-wise marshes. You can then build a gradually sloping rampart of sea-lavender or sea-wrack which will form a parapet sufficient to hide your head and shoulders from the oncoming skeins.

You can bow forward with your gun across your knees or, better still, laid ready in front of you, cocked, and with the barrel lightly covered with a strand or two of herbage which can be shaken off when you stand to take the shot. This point is important. Geese, as they come in, are continually scanning the ground in front of them and a pair of blued barrels will give your position away.

Gun-barrels camouflaged with paint would be ideal, but some-how one shrinks from painting a gun-barrel, and in any case it is harmful to the metal as rust can eat its way under a skin of paint and you can do nothing about it.

You can keep birds under observation as they are beating up for you by twisting your head sideways and watching them under the peak of your hat.

You can sometimes see them rise from the sands a mile or more away, so you have plenty of time. The face and hands should be camouflaged with daubs of mud. This again is most important, and how many fowlers do this! The light flesh tones show white from a long distance, as every army sniper knows.

Slowly the skein creeps up, now swinging left, now right, but (we hope) keeping a straight direction. Nearer it comes, those wide, beating wings enlarging as they approach, until the leader of the skein vanishes out of sight behind the peak of your hat. Then, and then only, can you stand up. Do not do this hastily, but take your time, a controlled, smooth movement is what is wanted, shaking the gun clear of the strand of sea-blite as you swing it up. By then the birds are passing directly over, and make sure you choose a goose which is not yet directly over your head. If you pick the right moment (and this takes some practice), the skein may not see you at all until you fire.

Immediately you have fired, each bird in the skein tips up on its tail, climbing to gain height and, at the same moment, breaking formation. It is amazing how quickly geese can do this. If you watch them going in some distance from your ambush, you will see just how far they can jump when shot at from the ground.

Very often you notice distant birds going in at dawn and see them all tip up their chins and climb—for no apparent cause—then a second or two later the sound of a shot reaches you.

In overhead birds, swing smoothly and get on your bird, bring the barrels forward until your target is hidden by the swinging barrels. Then press the trigger as the gun is still moving. If you have the bird in range, he is yours, and the next thing you will know is probably the resounding thump as he hits the merse behind you.

Your second shot at the 'jumping' skein will need little lead, not nearly so much as your first shot, and you can, as a rule, practically aim directly at your climbing target, though there is, of course, still a slight forward allowance to be made.

Geese coming in left or right present the same set of rules, but hold well up on your bird. Geese nearly always see you when they come in at an angle to your hide. As soon as you rise to your feet, they will spot you and will climb as surely as if you had shot at them. So you must bear this in mind and not err in giving too great a lead unless they have a wind behind them.

There is one 'almost overhead' shot which many fowlers find extraordinarily difficult, and it is one of the commonest. This is when the skein is coming over at an angle, possibly with a side wind. The geese are driving forward and at the same time *sideways*, so you have to swing both upwards and sideways. Very many birds are missed in this way. You remember to swing upwards but forget the side drift, and if the geese have seen you they will tip away from you, allowing the wind to help their progress.

A field ambush, the dyke inland, or the hide built against the fence, is always a simpler matter to construct, but not always so easy to make inconspicuous. Though you yourself may be completely hidden from incoming skeins, they will spot a suspicious mass against a fence and will give it a wide berth.

The dyke ambush is better, but geese again make it a golden

rule to keep clear of dykes and usually choose a very large field where they can side slip in to the centre.

In a case like this, when there is not a chance of a fence hide, then they may be shot by digging a pit in the middle of the field (and what farmer in his senses would consent to that?), or by matting covers. But such methods are elaborate and cumbersome.

2. Decoying

I have never quite made up my mind about decoying geese. That it is effective at times is beyond dispute, and this applies especially to the early part of the season. Pinks will sometimes be drawn to stuffed pinks, but I don't think they will come to stuffed greys. Greys will certainly come to stuffed pinks, for I have seen them actually pitch among them.

I always think that if you must decoy, it is essential to use stuffed birds, for the decoys must be as realistic as possible. I have seen painted wooden greylags (indeed I saw one only the other day in Bland's shop in London) and it may well be that a really good model is effective. But they are very costly and I should imagine a stuffed goose is much lighter to carry. Even so, a single stuffed decoy is of little use: the more you have, the better.

The actual stuffing, if you cannot cope with this yourself, must be left to a taxidermist, but it will be a costly business, and it may run you into five pounds a bird, perhaps more. But, with care, stuffed decoys last for years. Mac, who is a keen decoyman, will never travel far without his Pandora's box, as I call it, in which he keeps his 'coys. Mac is a methodical person and has devised a cunning way of detaching the legs. These screw into the bird when it is taken from the box and each foot has a spike which is pushed into the ground. Needless to say, the decoys must always be placed head to wind and as far as possible from your ambush. The idea is, of course, to attract the geese in range. When the skeins are flying in at dawn, some of them will quarter the fields looking for a suitable place to feed. This may take the skeins upwards of half an hour before they finally cautiously spiral down to alight in the centre of a stubble or pasture.

Other skeins which have fixed ideas of feeding and have probably found a safe harbour (they usually 'work' a stubble out in three days), will fly straight and high. These travelling geese may sometimes be attracted. You yourself should be well hidden in a dyke or against a fence and never be too eager to shoot. The skeins will circle a field for ten minutes sometimes before swinging in range. Their eyesight is acutely sharp, and I believe they can see other feeding gaggles far below them on the ground as keenly as a vulture can spot a carcase from afar.

I have tried, when decoying in this way, setting up geese which have already fallen to my gun, for when the fowl are plentiful and the morning propitious, you may sometimes bag more than a dozen birds. But dead birds propped up with a stick under the chin act as scarecrows, and I have never known them, in my experience at any rate, to be of any service. For one thing, your stuffed decoy stands well off the ground and is erect. The dead bird is of course 'sitting down' with only its head erect.

I think actually that decoying is a little unsporting. If there is no chance of a goose on the shore and you want to try it out, then do so, but I always feel it is not quite 'playing the game'.

Experienced fowlers are clever at 'calling' geese, or 'shouting a goose' as it's called by the Norfolk and Lincolnshire fowlers. I have called geese in myself both with wooden lures and with the mouth, and sometimes this is very effective. But I can never rid myself of the thought, as I see the distant goose wheeling round to my call, 'this is a bit caddish, somehow', and I think most fowlers will understand this viewpoint.

Sometimes decoying can be deadly dull, and I dislike being marooned in the middle of arable lands with nothing to watch but larks and hares. Nevertheless, some of the Highland peasantry kill a number of geese in this way on Saturday afternoons, and I suppose it is no more boring than a blank day's fishing.

3. *Punting*

Let me say at once I know very little about punting and now, I'm afraid, I've reached an age when the hazards and discomforts of hours afloat in the gunning-punt do not commend themselves to me. It calls for great skill and hardihood, much more than shore shooting, though I doubt whether the actual discharge of a punt-gun into a large mass of geese or duck would give me much pleasure—if any. Though the precise moment of firing calls for nice judgement, and the actual getting up to the fowl is a very skilled operation indeed, I cannot believe there is much satisfaction in firing a big gun 'into the brown', not knowing how many birds you may kill or how many will have to be finished off with the cripple stopper. There is too much of the butcher in this latter business. It would be a different matter if every bird was clean killed: even then it would not give me a great sense of achievement.

Now, of course, the punter is up in arms at once and says that the shore gunner also wounds a great many birds which go away to die lingering deaths. This also is true to a lesser extent. If a punter and a shore shooter compared notes on actual kills and 'bungled' shots over an entire season (and if they were really honest about it) the puntsman would find that he had wounded more birds, and indeed killed more. "Yes," he will say, "that may or may not be so, but when *I* wound a bird it is finished off with the cripple stopper whilst yours frequently flies off to the tide or comes down in some dyke and you never get it."

The average shot, however, should kill outright three out of five birds within range of him and certainly, shooting on the coast alone, he would do exceptionally well to average one goose a week, which makes sixteen geese, let us say, for the operative season. The puntsman may get sixteen at one discharge, though it is usually five or six, counting the cripples. He has only to have three successful outings and he has shot more than the shore shooter, and if a puntsman has only three successful shots in an entire working season, then he cannot be much of a puntsman.

Wildfowl are terrified of these big guns and an estuary which is often shot by punters will soon be cleared of fowl and the shore shooter will not have his fair share of sport.

4. *Driving*

This is one of the most uncertain forms of goose-shooting. You may spend an hour, perhaps two, in getting to a good inter-ception point between the geese and where you think they will go, and when your friend puts up the gaggles they will go in the opposite direction. Success can be achieved sometimes (as the reader shall learn), but goose-driving is very chancy work, at times most exciting and entertaining, at others most disappointing, with a waste of strenuous effort. It is well to remember that geese, like all birds, will rise into the wind. Their route out from the chosen pasture will usually steer clear of trees, dykes, and stacks, though even this cannot be held as a golden rule.

However, when a stalk is not possible, then by all means try a drive, but take your time over it. Give the gun plenty of law to reach his chosen spot, which must be agreed beforehand, and make as wide a detour as possible when you work round the geese. Never walk directly at them. The wind is the most important factor, its strength and direction must be carefully noted, and it goes without saying that the ambushing gunner must conceal himself as well as he can.

5. *Stalking*

Perhaps one of the most exciting forms of goose-shooting. I know no satisfaction so great as achieving success after a long and arduous stalk which has taken possibly a couple of hours. Perhaps the stalker gets the same satisfaction when he bags a fine stag.

An enormous amount of woodcraft, or rather 'field' craft is necessary. You must not mind getting wet and frozen; you must be prepared to take your time over it and never be hurried. Often when you are within an ace of success, when your finger is feeling for the trigger, some unforeseen happening will upset the whole show: an aeroplane drones over, a farm-hand passes along the next headland, a frightened hare which has seen you in the dyke makes away across the field, a distant shot—there are so many things which can make all your efforts come to nothing.

There are a few tips which I would give to those who like goose-stalking.

One is that geese, when feeding in a large gaggle, tend to feed upwind and they may stray within range of the boundary, whether that boundary be hedge, dyke or fence. They will then turn and walk back, though I have known them fly back, to the far end and work up-wind again if there is a strong breeze blowing.

I believe that the hearing of a goose is almost as keen as his eyesight. I do not believe they have much sense of smell, if any. I can hear many professional fowlers snort at this, but I only give my opinion. Men have been in hides dug in the middle of the feeding grounds and geese have been feeding all round them and have noticed nothing. Deer would not do this, nor would the humble rabbit, which has a very keen smell sense, as any rabbit-stalker with his ·22 has found when creeping up to a summer rabbit out at feed.

I have stalked geese at dawn as they rested on the tide edge, and there again you have to be prepared to take anything up to an hour over the messy job of getting within that vital 60 yards. A calm, frosty morning is useless for a marsh stalk, and wind is essential; nor are they so wary in a wind for some reason: maybe because they have to be careful to keep head on to the blast, and the noise of wind and wave, of course, drowns all other sounds. The roar of breakers and the continuous babbling among the ranks of the gaggle itself all help the fowler creeping up the dyke. In frost every movement you make is noisy, and a hard morning is usually very still.

So much for the various methods. But the best of all is, as I have said, the ambush in the dyke at break o' day when, for a preliminary delight, you have the glory of the dawn, a wonder which never palls. Those two hours from 7 to 9 a.m. on a winter's morning are worth all the others in the twenty-four.

12. *Wildfowl and Weather*

HARD frost following a thick fog transforms the coastal marshes. The tall reeds which fringe the edge of the estuary carry a fur of ermine whiteness and each tall stem, eight feet or more in height, bows over, its plumed seed head heavily weighed down under crystals of ice.

One such evening I went down to the shore, and never have I seen the firth so dramatic and sinister. Actually this particular highland firth is not extensive, and in normal weather is in nowise a creepy place. Even on the blackest night of storm it is not hostile, and only once have I had there that nameless panic which has come upon me about three times in my fowling career. This feeling is not an uncommon one to all those who frequent wild places alone and is, I understand, most noticeable on Dartmoor. I have had it once on the Wash and once or twice on the Solway, invariably when I have been far from the sea-wall and out on the sands or muds.

The only time I experienced it on this particular firth was, strangely enough, on a night of bright moonlight. I was standing at the end of a long corridor in the tall reed beds and it was a very still night of frost, the time about two in the morning. I was, of course, alone and had not even my dog with me. I do not think one can ever get that panic when one has a dog as a companion, at least I have yet to experience it.

Whether it was the sight of that long, black passage through the reeds, gashed here and there with bright patches of moonlight, or the complete and frightening silence, I do not know, but a name-less fear crept about me and possessed me, and I could stay there no longer.

On another evening when I went down to the frozen shore there was a sense of wonder, and even awe. The fog over the water was an opaque bronze tint which lightened only a little in the upper atmosphere. Visibility was not more than twenty yards at the most, though this changed a little now and again; sometimes I could see quite thirty yards, and then the murk would roll in again. Against this sombre wall of fog the white-furred reeds stood out in a pattern of wondrous beauty, each individual arched over, and wherever I looked, within the range of vision these white hoops surrounded me.

I knew that inland of me there was a large party of greylags feeding on a stubble. I had seen them there before the fog shut down and I guessed that if they did not flight in before the fog became too thick, they would most likely stay where they were until dusk.

I made my way through the frozen reeds, and every step brought down a rustling cascade of ice particles which soon covered my coat and hat with a similar fur, so that I must have looked like a walking ghost. I was so familiar with this section of the marsh that I knew I could not get lost as long as I kept the dim loom of the outermost reed wall in sight, and as it grew dark I intended moving back to the edge of these tall reeds and the entrance to the path.

I picked my way across the mud, which was quite soft, for the frost had not had sufficient time to harden it, and finding a shallow gutter I sat down on my sit-bag. There was no need to attempt concealment. The geese would never see me until they were in range, so I knew that any dim shape with wide-flapping wings was mine if I held the gun straight.

How quiet it was out there on the edge of the tide with the fog hemming me in on all sides! Now and again I heard the feeble 'seep peep' of little waders close at hand and occasionally a whistle of wings went by, though I could see nothing. This wall of whiteness about me was so uniform it was difficult to say where the sun was going down, for there was no trace of any brightening of the fog in that direction.

As flight time drew near, the whole scene darkened and the fog became thicker. There was still no sign nor sound of the geese. Just when I thought of rising and making my way back to the tall reeds, I heard faint and far off the clamour of the greys. It was foolish of them to advertise their coming, but no doubt they cry to one another in thick weather so as to keep in touch.

The sound drew nearer and nearer until, without the slightest warning, a great mass of gliding, grey silhouettes appeared over my head. Swinging up my gun, I brought the leader crashing down.

The fog I have described lasted for two days, and the following morning at flight time I was again out on the marshes, only a little lower down. Geese never moved until quite late, and it was almost ten o'clock before I heard them on the wing. These were pinks, and several large parties went inland fairly close to me, though I never saw them; all I could hear was the swish of their wings in the murk and an occasional yelp.

Then a large skein suddenly loomed overhead. Again I was lucky and brought down the leader, and I should have had another but on the shot the geese "sat on their tails" and vanished in the mist.

The sudden way that geese will appear out of fog invariably takes the fowler by surprise, even though he may hear them coming from some way off and is, in a sense, prepared for the encounter.

These days of fog are not common after Christmas. On the western seaboard the weather is usually calm, frosty, and bright. Though this type of weather is poor for wildfowling, it is nevertheless very pleasant to be out all day on the marshes in bright sun, and there is never a dull moment to the man who likes watching birds as well as shooting them.

I have seen hen harriers and waxwings in such clear frosty weather and some of the rarer waders, though this particular firth is poor for waders.

I always favour an average open winter for wildfowling and I have always had more sport then than during extremes of weather. Nevertheless, during hard, continuous frost on the Solway in 1950, some friends of mine shot a good many geese by building hides of ice blocks out on the tide-line. At that time I was farther north and I had very poor sport indeed as all the birds had moved south. I believe that great numbers of geese were also congregating on the Severn during that particular hard spell.

Cold weather certainly tames geese, and I think that greylags especially are apt to come more to decoys in snowy weather. I will give one instance of this.

For a week or more we had had much frost and snow, though the latter was never deep. It was sufficient to cover the fields to a depth of an inch or so, and geese, both pinks and greys, were coming to a clover field on a certain Scottish farm.

We had obtained permission to try for them and had accordingly built hides in a dyke which formed the northern boundary. This dyke was deep and, what was more important, tolerably dry. Very little work with a bill-hook was sufficient to construct some substantial and comfortable ambushes. All this work was carried out one afternoon, and next morning, before it was light, Mac, Bill, and myself were in position, with decoys set out on the stubble about forty yards distant in the snow.

There was mist at dawn, which increased to a fog by sunup

with visibility about forty yards, an ideal morning. Every twig was covered in rime, for it was still freezing, though the fog foretold a temporary thaw.

Fairly late I heard geese moving and a very large skein of pinks came in, passing behind us and heading for the hills. Though they must have seen the decoys, they went straight on and never altered course, and I only had a dim glimpse of them.

Soon after, I heard greylags croaking. They had been coming to this stubble for several days and had not been disturbed. These geese came sailing out of the fog with paddles down and landed all round the decoys: one even pitched in the middle of them!

Mac had a shot with his eight-bore and knocked out two, but they were too far off for me, so I held my fire.

Half an hour passed without any sight or sound, then a small party came in on my left and swung over the decoys giving me a stern shot (always a deadly one if geese are in range), and I dropped a very big old gander at seventy-five paced yards with BB shot. The bird just packed up and never stirred again, which shows what this heavy shot can do when it gets home in a vital place.

We had one other bird off this field before the sun dispersed the fog, but the geese did not come back for a second dose and forsook the field for the remainder of our stay.

This particular farm is a good one for both pinks and greys, though the favourite field is of great size. Unless the weather was thick, it was difficult to get a shot.

I remember one successful stalk, however, on this same farm, and this took place on another occasion and on an afternoon of sun. It was so warm that midges danced in front of me as I lay behind a low bank bordering the field, while Bill 'bellied' out from the stack-yard of the farm and took up a position behind some dead ground between the geese and the sea. Mac made a long detour and came up on the north boundary of the field.

When driving geese, the 'driver' should never walk directly at the gaggle but walk up and down on the far side of them. The geese, if they are feeding in a large field, will not rise at once but will slowly walk away, only to rise when they feel the distance is getting dangerous.

In this case they allowed Mac to come within 200 yards before taking off, and the whole skein of about thirty greylags went in right over Bill, who was lying behind some dead grass with his eight-bore. He stood up and had a couple of shots, bringing down the leader, which was one of the largest greys I have seen shot.

13. *Watch Your Step*

THE dangers of wildfowling can be exaggerated; they can also be underrated. Fox-hunting, mountaineering, pot-holing, ski-ing, sailing, all have an element of risk. After all, what sport is worth while if it hasn't?

Punting to wildfowl, as I have said, can be a highly dangerous business. Even experienced men sometimes get into trouble, and I doubt whether there is a single puntsman who has not, at some time or another, had a narrow escape.

The danger to the shore shooter is not half so great, but at the same time we have all had our exciting and, maybe, unpleasant moments. I have never been stuck, badly stuck that is, in a quicksand, though I've been lost in fog on the marshes, as readers of my former book, *Tide's Ending*, will remember.

My friend Robin once had a nasty experience. I'm going to tell you about it because Robin can't write a word himself. If he chose, he could write several books of his adventures, though they would not be worth reading. Robin is just lacking in any imagination. Perhaps that's why he runs into trouble from time to time. Most unimaginative people cannot see more than one jump ahead, though, in a crisis, when trouble does come, they can deal with it calmly and with courage, which is just what Robin does. Incidentally, he will be mad with me for telling this story, it may even harm our friendship, but I'll take the risk. I shall tell it as he told it to me, for, like a lot of people, he can describe his experiences graphically enough but cannot put them down on paper.

But first let me say something about the risks which the shore shooter has to face. I must always bear in mind I may be talking to someone who knows nothing at all about wildfowling and is reading about it for the first time. There's a likelihood for—I was going to say, the expert, but modesty forbids—a likelihood, I say, in writing above the head of the non-fowling fraternity.

For instance, when I speak of 'greys' and 'pinks', sea pies, knot, plickplack, and 'blackbacks', the reader will wonder what on earth I'm talking about. It is because of this I think it best to put a glossary of terms at the end of this book so that if you are puzzled you can 'look it up'.

Most of that area between the tides is either sand, ooze, or open, flat marsh. Sand is harmless enough and very nice to walk on, but it is sometimes 'quick', and a bad quicksand is worse than deep mud (which can be most frightening but not often dangerous), and it's worse getting into one than losing oneself in a fog, or being cut off by the tide, or having your punt sink under you. If you are lost, you can move around, you are at least mobile, and a compass will usually see you out by the back door. If you are cut off by the tide, there are two alternatives open to you: either swimming (and nobody who goes fowling should be unable to swim) or making such a noise that someone will notice your predicament and come and take you off.

If your punt sinks under you, you are again mobile, for a certain limited time at any rate. But if a quicksand grabs you, you can't do much about it; you certainly can't get out if you've gone well in, and it's quite a job for anyone else to get you out.

The chances are there won't be anyone else. Robin was lucky, or he wouldn't be alive today thirsting for my blood. Most years wild‑fowlers get into trouble. In the winter of 1939 two lost their lives on the Tay. It is the most dangerous form of shooting.*

Two things you've got to watch: the tide, and your step. Look after these and you'll be unharmed. I never trust the sea; no island dweller ever does. It's sly, it's immensely strong, though you wouldn't think it when you see it lazy and silver on a calm winter's day of sun and frost, or August blue.

I shall tell this story as Robin told it to us in the snug bar of a certain pub which is familiar to many fowlers, both professional and amateur, on the Scotch side of the Solway.

We were swopping yarns, Robin, myself, and a stranger who had dropped into the bar. Robin had had a few drinks, which was all to the good, because when he's dead sober he doesn't say much. The third member of the party had been bragging a bit of how, in company with another, he'd killed a cart‑load of wigeon on the Essex marshes. His pal had got stuck in a soft place and had to be pulled out and was very scared about the whole business, so much so he'd never gone fowling again.

Robin took a pull at his tankard. "I can understand that, you know."

"Rot", said the stranger. "Sheer funk and panic! You can always get out of a bad place if you're stuck."

Robin shook his head. "You can't always get out, you know, not by yourself. I'll tell you what happened to me. It was just after the war. I'd been looking forward to a bit of fowling ever since the show started, for, unlike a lot of R.A.F. chaps, I didn't have a chance of doing much shooting, except at Jerries. Then they sent me to Canada to train air crews and, though I managed to get in a bit of duck‑shooting on the lakes, it wasn't fowling, not proper fowling as we know it.

"When I was in the R.A.F. I used to look at a map sometimes

91

* Apart from farmers' hare shoots

when I had a quiet hour, a map of our own coast-line at home, and go over all the ground I'd shot in the old days, sometimes alone and sometimes with "B.B." here.

"I'd never done any fowling in Wales and there was one little bit on the West Coast [Robin did not say exactly where because no good fowler ever gives away the name of a good locality] which took my fancy. It looked a 'goosey' sort of place, if you know what I mean. I can sort of smell geese by even looking at a map, if you get my meaning.

"So when I came out of the R.A.F. I went down there. I felt I deserved a break and it's always interesting to try new ground. I had my gratuity money like the other chaps. Some spent it on drink, women, or chicken farming—things like that. I spent mine (or some of it) on this little trip to Wales and buying a new Magnum. It's a Bland, and cost a packet, but a peach of a gun: the first good one I've ever owned.

"I found a dirty little pub in a village within a couple of miles of the river mouth. It was kept by a nasty sort of devil who was hardly ever sober. He boozed half the night and never functioned until opening time next day.

"The beer was awful. They were rotten quarters really, and I've had a taste of a few. It was the bugs which really worried me, but there was nowhere else to stay, so I just had to make the best of it; with Keating's and the back of a hairbrush I managed to keep them under control . . . more or less.

"Of course, if it hadn't been for the fowling I'd have packed it in right away, but the shooting was really good there: whitefronts, of course, and plenty of wigeon. Best shore shooting at wigeon I'd ever had; even better than Scotland.

"It was a queer sort of place, sand dunes, you know, a lot of sand dunes with rushy marshes inshore of the dunes; reminded me a bit of Norfolk.

"The whitefronts rested on the sand-bars at the river mouth and came in at dawn over the dunes, low, too; looked to me as though nobody ever bothered about 'em. I only met one local chap. He was a type called Dai Jones, who sometimes went out after them. Dai was a typical Welshman: stocky, dark, round face, with a fund of the dirtiest stories I've ever heard, not even funny ones. He knew a bit about the shooting and, after a while, he came out with me and showed me the lie of the land.

"As a rule I don't like relying on local fowlers. I like to find my own way around and shoot the way I think the place ought to be shot, like 'B.B.' here. Maybe you think that's a bit stupid. Perhaps it is, but I'm the sort of chap who likes to do things off his own bat.

"Dai showed me where the best wigeon flighting was, and then left me to it. When I asked him if the sands were all right, he said they were and he'd never heard of anyone getting stuck, or any-thing like that, so it must have made me a bit careless. Just shows that you can't always believe what locals tell you. Maybe Dai never went out much on the sand. Now I come to think of it, he seemed to do all his shooting in the dunes.

"Actually, at that part of the coast, there are two rivers coming in to the sea, with a high mountain in between. A bit inland it's very pretty country, though I haven't much of an eye for scenery. The wigeon used to fly across from the sand-banks off the river's mouth and come over the dunes to the bay behind where there was plenty of fine salting grass. This is where the whitefronts came over too, when the wind was right—which wasn't often. Sometimes they went inland to the south and sometimes the other way, to the other river and the high sands to the west.

"Well, I'd been down there for a couple of nights and bagged about six wigeon and one whitefront, and then the moon began to go off and the wigeon weren't so hot. But more geese came in, and the weather turned a bit frosty but not hard enough to drive them away.

"One afternoon I went down to the dunes about a couple of hours before flight as I'd noticed a lot of curlew about. Curlew can be grand fun when the tide's making, as you know.

"I met Dai on the way down. He'd got the afternoon free: it was Saturday, and he seemed inclined to come along with me, but I put him off. I said I'd meet him after flight at the pub where I was staying and we'd have a few drinks. I didn't want to seem stand-offish. He went up the dunes to my right, and I went across the little marsh where the wigeon came to see if they'd been using it much lately under the moon. There was a packet of droppings and feathers round the flashes and I reckoned I might get a shot or two there later at sundown, though there wasn't any moon.

"So I went and sat down in the dunes and waited for flight time and the odd curlew. It had been a clear, bright afternoon, with a touch of frost, and I watched the sun go down over St. David's, a round, rose-red, frosty sort of sun like a Dutch cheese, with only a few clouds high up in the sky, sort of golden clouds like whisps of hair—cirrus cloud, it's called, and it only happens at anything from 20,000 feet up—and often in still, frosty weather.

"I'm not much of a hand at describing things, as I've told you chaps, but it was a jolly fine picture, that wide bay, all silvery, and the red sun glowing on the stretches of sand, turning them a wonderful rose-pink. Never seen anything like it.

"It was very still too, with just the sound of the sea on the bar and an occasional curlew calling. The tide was coming in and I could see the little wader trips on the move, leap-frogging back, you know how they do, one lot getting up and dropping behind the feeding flocks, and all the time the tide creeping and brimming along the little pans and flashes. When the tide comes sliding in over the flats, it's a different sea from the white breakers on the shore. They are noisy and honest, but the creeping tide's like a stalking cat.

"Once I heard a single shot away to my right, where Dai had gone, but he was a hell of a way off. I guessed he'd put up a rabbit in the dunes, or maybe a curlew.

"The sun went down behind the hills and a few curlew came yodelling out from the fields. It's odd how chill and grey the shore becomes when the sun dips behind the hills—just like someone pulling down a blind.

"Then I heard some whitefronts. You know what a musical, laughing sort of call they have, jolly attractive row, if you know what I mean, and soon I saw a little tangle coming in from the high country behind. They were a hell of a height and I thought they'd go right out into the bay. But whether it was anything to do with the making tide, I don't know, but they spiralled down: a treat to watch, especially if you've done any flying yourself—side-slipping, falling leaf stunt, right over the wigeon marsh. Blow me down if they didn't come sailing in over the dunes where I was, just as if they were offering me a special sitting chance. It was a piece of cake.

"I was so surprised, I muffed it. I should have had a right and left; as it was I only hit a bird on the left leg of the skein, and he wasn't killed outright. He came down with a broken wing and dunted the shore about sixty yards off. At first I thought he was dead, but when I walked out to get him (I hadn't a dog then), I saw he'd got his head up. When a goose has his head up it's wise to shoot again, but this chap didn't give me a chance but set off 'waddle pat' over the sand.

"I went after him of course. If I'd had my old Ben then he'd have had him in a jiffy. But this whitefront had a good start, and when he saw me running he ran too, helping himself along with his wings. The sand was hard enough and I gained on him. I thought I was in range to finish him off, so I stood still and had another shot, but you know how hard it is to judge the range. The pellets just pattered feebly round him like a summer shower.

That made him go all the faster, and I started after him again. I don't know if you've ever run a long way in fowling kit, but believe me it takes some doing. It puffs you as much as a good bout with the gloves. Soon I was blowing like a whale and that old whitefront was still toddling along just out of reach.

"Then I got on harder sand and made up the lost ground. I saw he was making for a narrow flash of water; it was really a tidal pan and the tide was just flooding into it, all pink in the sunset. My old whitefront was as black as a little nigger against the westward glow when my third shot sent him sprawling and flapping, to lie still on the other side, on a little island of sand not yet covered by the making tide.

"I was pleased about that, for it had been a hell of a run, and when I looked back I found I was about 500 yards from the dunes.

"I waded through the shallow water, which didn't come halfway up my legs, and then, as I reached the sand on the far side, I felt my feet sink a little. I was only a matter of ten feet from my goose. Another step and my right leg went in deep, up to the knee. I pressed down with my left foot and that went deeper too and I hardly shifted my right. I was trapped.

"I'd been in soft spots many times before and this was just annoying. Another couple of steps and the goose would have been in the bag. Now I was in it up to my thighs.

"There was nothing for it but to lie back. I put the gun under my shoulders and threw my body backwards, at the same time trying to draw my knees up. But the suction was too great, and with my exertions the dry surface around me was dry no longer. It became all smooth, almost oily. When I moved, a sluggish ripple rolled outwards. It held me as firmly as cement.

"To stand up now would be asking for trouble—to panic (and I don't mind telling you I began to feel mighty scared) would be the end of the business.

"For a moment or so I lay quite still, my shoulders pressing on my gun, which was of course now well down in the sand. I didn't seem to notice the icy wetness of my thighs and back.

"Ten feet away (I could just see it) was the white chest of the whitefront barred with black. The paddles were still giving a little kick every now and then. At last they were still.

"It looked as though my goose was cooked as well as his.

"I'd rest awhile and then have another spell of drawing my knees up. Stupidly, I'd padded the soles of my gutty boots with several wads of paper before I came out. Usually I have my waders on the loose side. To have your waders fitting too tightly is about on a par with riding a nervous horse in farm-boots with your feet well home in the stirrup. It's asking for trouble.

"I tried to figure things out, what would happen. I wasn't getting any nearer to freeing myself. If I could have worked my legs free I could have rolled out as I've done before now, but the trouble was the pressure of the sand was like a cold vice—it was quite a frightening pressure, almost like a tourniquet. Must have been the suction, I suppose.

"Well, there I was, stuck up to the thighs in the middle of a nasty patch of 'jelly' sand which had the consistency of cement. I thought of Peter Scott's story in his book *Morning Flight*, how a friend of his had been trapped in much the same way on a Scottish estuary. I knew the place. Only the fact that the salmon-fishing had started that day saved him, for some chappies in a boat came along and pulled him out.

"I tried, I say, to figure things out. My only hope was my chance meeting with Dai. When he didn't find me at the pub as we'd arranged he might wonder where I'd got to. But I figured that by the time he'd hung around wondering where I was, the tide would be eight feet over my head and they wouldn't find me until the next morning. Perhaps they wouldn't find me then, perhaps not ever.

"When I thought of that, I had my one and only moment of sheer terror. I yelled, or rather I opened my mouth to yell, but only a sort of cracked, hoarse scream came out. That sobered me up and made me damned ashamed of myself.

"I looked along my chest at the goose. He wasn't there. I raised myself a bit with my elbows on my gun, and then I saw him. He was now fifteen yards off, floating belly up and slowly going inshore. It still wanted half an hour to flight time, and there was plenty of light. I thought of shooting off my remaining cartridges. I had, as far as I could remember, about half a dozen in my belt, but I daren't try and pull the gun from under me. I was too scared. That one rigid bar, though it seemed deeper in now, was my last remaining hope of keeping on top of this stuff.

"There was one of those old blackbacks hanging around. I could hear it 'laughing', you know the row they make, sort of HA HA HA HA . . . HA HA HA HA. It must have been circling round for quite a time, for the sound came first in front and then from behind, and soon he took a turn right over me, and that made him croak some more. Miserable old buzzard! I've always hated those birds. I yelled at him and wished I could get at my gun.

"Water began spilling up the channel behind me now, with flat cakes of yellow foam on it, all travelling towards the shore like things on a conveyor belt. A flock of sea pies went over not more than ten feet off my head, all piping like blazes.

"I figured that in another half-hour the worst would be over, for I could hear the distant hiss of the tide coming at me over the flats. Then something made me look again towards the shore line and I saw Dai, it must be Dai, walking along in front of the dunes. I yelled then like a madman. Suppose I *was* mad by then, or jolly near it, but that little figure went on walking. It seemed to move ever so slowly, plod, plod, in the dry loose sand.

"This was my only hope, somehow I must attract his attention, and I'd have to fire my gun if I foundered in the process.

"I rolled over on my left elbow and the wet sand reached my chin. I twisted my right arm behind me and lugged on the gun, and the whole mess quivered like a giant jelly.

"Somehow I got my hand round the pistol grip and lugged, and by a tremendous effort I pulled the gun clear. I went down lower, which is what I expected would happen, but I'd got the gun clear, and even if Dai didn't hear me or see me, I'd be able to blow out my brains before the tide had done its horrid business.

"I washed two cartridges in the film of water which now surrounded me and thanked my stars they were waterproof. But I had the hell of a job to shut the gun-breech because of the sand.

"I got it shut, however, and let drive both barrels. I saw Dai stop and look. I raised my arm and waved my cap. Dai still stood shading his eyes with one hand. I could only just see him, but hoped I'd be outlined against the westward glow. Somehow I got two more shells in and shot those off too, bang! bang! and still Dai stood there like an old heron. I expect he was puzzled, because it must have been a job to see me.

"Then I had a brain-wave. On the right side of my belt I had one of those rocket cartridges Eleys made before the war. They may still make 'em, I don't know. The idea was that you could correct your aim by them, for you could follow the flight of the cartridge, rather like a miniature Very light.

"I pushed this in the left barrel and my last cartridge but one in the right. I fired the latter just as Dai started to walk on. I saw him pause again and look in my direction, and then I fired my rocket cartridge. It looked quite spectacular, hissing up into the evening sky where the first stars were showing, and Dai spotted me right away.

"I waved again and yelled for all I was worth, and he began

walking towards me. Then he broke into a run as the truth dawned on him.

"About five minutes later he was on the other side of the runnel, which was a few yards wider now and getting wider every minute.

"Dai had an old Magnum; a terrible old thing. It had been a good gun once, but he'd neglected it. It had a hole in one barrel about half-way down, and every time he fired it a jet of smoke came out. Dai said this barrel killed better than the other—usual sort of twaddle these chaps talk about their guns. He'd a leather sling fitted to it—God knows why. The only slings I've ever seen on guns are on eight-bores and German hunting-rifles.

"He unclipped this and chucked it across to me, and somehow I got it round my body under the arm-pits, after letting it out as far as it would go. Then Dai edged as near as he dared to come and reached out his gun stock and I buckled the strap through the trigger-guard. Then began a sort of pull devil pull baker, but my boots held me; apart from nearly pulling me in two and Dai going in himself up to the knees, we didn't make any progress.

"Then Dai fumbled in his pocket and produced a fearsome jack-knife. I'd seen him gutting a rabbit with this knife in the dunes the day before, and it was razor sharp.

"He told me to try and slit my gutty boots up the front from the inside. This wasn't so easy as it sounds, but I worked the knife down as far as I could, leaning back as much as possible and ripping at the rubber.

"All this time the tide was sliding round us. It seemed to be loosening the sand a bit, for I could feel the suction getting less. When I'd slit my boots as low as I could, Dai lugged again on the gun barrel, trying to pull me backwards. At last I felt my legs give a bit inside the boots. Another pull from Dai and I rolled out. A moment later I was back on the firm sand with no boots or stockings, for those were still in the sand. I was lucky to save my gun. I even got my goose, which was a bit of triumph. It had floated in, of course, and we picked it up along the shore on the way home!"

Robin pushed his tankard across. "Same again, Jamie . . . wonder why you can't get a real honest pint north of the Border!"

14. *Stalking in the Snow*

THE fowler who lives far from the coast has one great disadvantage. He cannot grasp the opportunity of suitable weather. The man who lives on the spot can pick and choose his day, provided of course he can afford the time. But who, in these days, is a man of leisure?

At the same time, I believe that if we could go wildfowling whenever we wished, and for as long as we wished, we should perhaps not relish our trips so much. It is the hardworking man who can only afford, say, a week or ten days during the short season, or even a couple of week-ends, who really enjoys the sport to the full. I know it is so in my case. It cannot be nearly so much fun, for instance, to be born to wealth and leisure, as to gain those desirable things by one's own efforts, though I fear that this is becoming increasingly difficult these days when incentive and skill do not bring the rewards they deserve. The principle that the lazy and bad worker should be paid at the same rate as the industrious and skilled severs the very root of healthy endeavour. Competition is nothing to be ashamed of; it is a healthy spur. In these days it seems ambition is a crime.

But this is no place for airing politics, heaven forbid! What I wish to do is to take you with me for two days to a certain northern firth and that you should share with me my experiences.

The time is January 1951, and the date the 9th. Weather: clear, very frosty, and bright sun all day.

Snow covered the fields, but only thinly. It had drifted a little in the hollows and steep burn banks. First, then, Tuesday, the 9th of January.

The alarm clock went off at 6.30. Those who have been on similar expeditions will know very well the reactions to the sound of the alarm clock. For the first few days of a fowling trip its insistent shrilling summons is obeyed with alacrity. But as the days go on the response is not so immediate; by the end of the trip everyone is inclined to linger for as long as possible between warm blankets. The fact is the body protests vehemently against being hauled from bed; when awakened by the alarm the delicious warmth and sense of langour seem to be intensified and those last few snatched minutes are indeed greatly prized. Even the prospect of a good flight is not, for a minute or two, powerful enough to make you leap from bed. And then your imagination gets busy. You smell the cold dawn wind and hear the rustle of the reeds. You hear also the geese calling on the tide, and soon in your mind's eye the black, wavering line of birds flogging up for your hide. As the seconds pass such mental pictures are not to be borne, you must be there.

So on this morning all these familiar things followed one another in ordered sequence, and at last, with a spring, I was out of bed.

In the fire place was a heap of dead ash, a single red coal gleamed when I raked it aside, and upon it I put some rolled paper balls, a stick or two, and soon a cheerful blaze sprang up. As it grew in warmth and stature, I pulled on my trousers, calling to the others to get up too. Tony was out of bed at once, but Mac tried to put us off with a grunt and had to be roused a second time.

We gulped down some hot, sweet tea from the waiting thermos

and munched some biscuits, dressing as we did so. The time it takes to array oneself in fowling gear is considerable. The long gutty boots which have been drying all night in the hearth are pulled on after new newspaper soles have been inserted. The sweaters are pulled over heads, cartridge-belts buckled round waists, outer coats are struggled into, and mittens pulled on. One needs all these to combat the polar cold of the marshes on a January morning.

All is ready, the last cup of tea is drained and we step out into the cobbled yard. There has been a heavy frost which has formed a white fur all over the bonnet of the van and the radiator rug.

Mac gets in and switches on the dash-board light, and soon the starter grinds. The engine fires after a decent interval, the exhaust puffs dense and white on the polar air.

Stars shine brightly overhead, the big beeches behind the inn are motionless, for there is no wind. Away to the east there is already a pale flush of light.

Down the hill, turn left, and then the long, straight road which leads to the sea-wall. As we go I can hear the crackle-crackle of ice on the road and now and again the stern of the van swings a little. Then the line of oaks, then the cottage where the 'horraman' lives (what a horraman is, I haven't the vaguest idea), and a lamp is throwing a bright glow on the ceiling. More oaks—and then, at last, the gateway where the van pulls in and we tumble out.

Lights are switched off, snap, snap; one's world darkens to its true tonal values, and Mac locks the back of the van. A moment later we are through the wire and are tramping over the field behind the sea-wall. The frozen snow crunches and squeaks under our big boots; that is the only sound, scrunch, scrunch, as six booted feet propel their owners goosewards.

No word is spoken. When one approaches the sea-wall, conversation seems to lapse and the ear is all the time alert for sounds from the sea.

There is a faint gabbling to the northwards as we stand in the gateway at the top of the bank close to the dense bushes of broom. The icy air fills the lungs so that it almost hurts to breathe, but it is scented with the reeds and the sea—that land 'between the tides'.

We talk in whispers. Mac first. "They're down at Leaning Buoy this morning!"

Myself: "Sounds to me like the Long Breakwater."

Tony: "Let's try Leaning Buoy. I'll go north of it towards the Long Breakwater."

"And I'll keep this side," I say. (It won't be such a long tramp for me after flight—regular old soldier!)

Mac decides on the middle beat, and we set off along the bank. It is rough going for there is still very little light, though the snow makes things more plain. I reach my steps in the bank and, with a whispered "Good luck, Mac", I clamber down to the reeds whilst the dark figures of my two companions vanish in the darkness. I can hear their crunching feet for a long time. That is the worst of a frosty, still morning: every small sound is telegraphed to the sharp ears of the geese should they be resting on the tide edge.

This morning the tide wants another hour to flood, but it will not reach the high reeds. I see my path white against the dun forest of reed. It winds like a rabbit's track, now this way, now that, and my boots slip and slide. In open weather these tracks through the reeds are miry, one sinks in to the calf, making a fearful row. But now all moisture is locked fast, progress is silent and rapid. The reeds grow taller. They brush my cheek, sending down icy particles of frost which lodge between my coat collar and neck.

I reach the edge of the merse where the tall reeds end and the short stuff begins. Beyond that is the 'plickplack', the open muds sparsely covered with spiky tufts of reed. It is there the geese may be resting, though sometimes they are right inshore on the fringe of the high reeds.

When I reach the edge of the tall beds I stop and listen carefully for three minutes or more. There is no sound opposite, all is silence, not even a wader 'peeps'.

Cautiously I move outwards from the tall stuff, and now it is not easy to walk in silence. Here and there are hidden gutters, some over five feet deep, and the mud in them, down below there, never freezes even in the hardest weather. It is up these narrow creeks the tides ebb and flow once every twelve hours as regularly as the swing of a pendulum.

Somewhere in the darkness, a hundred yards ahead, is my favourite little creek. It is about four feet deep and very narrow. The short reeds form grand cover; I can sit down there on my goose bag well screened from the sharpest eyes.

I move slowly outwards, placing each foot carefully, for I wish to make the least possible noise. And then—there is a tornado of cackling and threshing of wings. A big party of greylags lift on my left, well behind me. If I had only known they were there! They have been roosting well up near the tall reeds and I have missed a chance! I catch a glimpse of a wing going up and down, but I do not fire. How can one judge the range? They may have been forty, seventy, or even eighty yards distant.

I hear them cackling away as they swing out into the firth, and others raise their voices to left and right along the edge of the tide. Fully five minutes the clamour goes on, becoming fainter as the birds go out to the sea, and again silence falls.

My gutter is reached; by instinct, almost, I have come straight to it. There I sit down, warm with my exertions, despite the bitter morning. And now follows over half an hour of comparative silence. The light in the east grows every moment and soon details of marsh and reed bed fall into their appointed places.

Strange, black objects which might be geese or tussocks of reed become visible. Gulls begin to call, a curlew or two crying thinly to the icy dawn. Far up river a confused murmur of goose voices breaks out and for some minutes this goes on, sounding now loud, now faint, like the cheering of a football crowd, as a big pack swings about over the sands, disturbed maybe by some gunner a mile or more from me.

A distant shot sounds far away, then the faint double 'blump, blump' of a double eight. There is no sound from Tony or Mac. When and if they fire, I shall hear them plainly.

The light grows bright now and the mountains swim sharp and clear against the paleness of the sky. Against that paleness, nebulous shapes pass along, strings of gulls going up river and maybe a close, black bunch of duck; mallards whistle in. Suddenly it is morning, with the calm estuary shining like a sword.

A few geese go in to right and left, high and purposeful, flying without sound. It looks like a blank flight. By 8.30 a.m. all my surroundings are visible, the white frost furred on every reed. Nothing comes my way. Then a skein of pinks appear in sight, coming high from down river. They swing in over Mac, and he does not fire, wise man! Turning in my gutter I watch them go, clear in the pellucid morning light, bound for the frozen fields, where—who knows?

Then distant cackling and here come a party of seven greylags. They head in from the shore straight for where I judge Tony to be. I watch them closely. Suddenly every bird towers. One black speck drops, down, down, and then I hear two shots. Tony at least has got his bird.

The flight is over. There is that undefinable something which tells me this. Good fowlers always know when the time has come to 'pack up'. I have noticed again and again how sometimes at dawn or evening flight all the guns meet simultaneously at the car, having started to walk back at the same time. The inexperienced fowler will sometimes stay on long after there is a chance of a shot and so keep the other guns waiting.

At morning flight when the time comes to leave the shore it is amusing to watch one's fellow guns emerge from hiding. When the flight is at its height no figures are to be seen; only distant shots tell you other guns are in your territory. But as the light grows, tiny black knobs appear over dyke and reed bed, stealthily emerging like some species of beetle or rail.

Soon small, black figures may be seen standing heron-wise about the gutters, but should a goose appear they scuttle like bugs for hiding.

This stealthy emergence always amuses me and it is one of the features of dawn flighting.

When the bright sun topped the mountains I walked along the plickplack and joined up with Mac, who had not had a shot. Together we walked to Tony's post and found him struggling desperately among the tall reeds. His bird had fallen some eighty yards from where he stood, right into the tall stuff. Somewhere it was lying there. Not even my labrador Judy could face that dense, brittle forest where old reeds lie in tangled breastworks. And until long after flight time we searched, tramping back and forth among the frozen reeds, the white rime powder falling down into our boot-tops. But we never found Tony's goose, and it was a sorrowful party which returned to the waiting van. All the bustle of the day had begun now and much of the magic had gone from the scene.

Carts moved about the fields, manure heaps steamed, trains whistled, and Postie could be seen wheeling his bicycle along the icy lane because he dared not ride it.

So much for flight on January 9th.

That afternoon, after a good lunch, we set out again, not for the marshes, but for Puddy Tat Hill. Mac was unable to come as he had business to do in the distant city, whither he had gone by train. So it was Tony and me.

The sun still shone and the snow glistened. The lovely lady at the farm was not visible to cheer us, but the greylags were! A party of twenty or so were busy feeding on the south sunny slope of Puddy Tat Hill, feeding as unconcernedly as chickens. It was a lovely stalk. I thought of Mac and what he was missing!

We left the van in the stack-yard and tramped out across the snowy field to the foot of the hill. Half-way up we went to our knees and crawled, side by side like bears, slower and slower as we neared the crest.

Ahead was a wire fence. Dead buff grass, crisped with rime, formed a fringe, and behind this we bellied along and then lay down, not daring to peep over.

For several minutes we lay thus getting our breath, for bellying any distance can be very hard work. I looked behind us. There lay the flat fields stretching to the burn and some rooks were clustered blackly beside some stacks where pigeons wheeled and fluttered.

In the middle of one vast field was one small, black, moving spot. It was a hare. She was running in circles. Then she headed our way. For five minutes I watched her come with growing interest and amusement. Nearer, nearer, until the little rufus-coated animal was at the base of Puddy Tat Hill. She ascended with a rocking motion, coming directly for us as if drawn by a magnet.

And in a minute or so she came up the fence and passed within four feet of us, her wide, black eyes showing no suspicion, no fear. Then she sat up with twitching whiskers and gazed at the white ridge. Perhaps she could hear the geese.

For a moment she hopped around like a tame rabbit sniffing the snow, and then, as if an idea had occurred to her, she went bobbing over the ridge.

My gun was cocked and so was Tony's. I had BB shot in both barrels; so had he.

A second after the hare tittupped from view, four heads, sur-mounting long sinuous necks, shot up over the white rim in front. The greylags had seen the hare, which must have lolloped right through the gaggle. And as those sharp, little, brown eyes stared point-blank at our fence the great birds sprang upwards, for they saw us at once.

Bang! Bang! Bang! Bang! Four barrels went off. The whole hill-side seemed to spout geese. The bird I fired at staggered and dropped to the snow. There it rolled, over and over down the white frozen slope, and a moment later I was holding it by the paddles, watching the geese swing away for the misty firth. More geese must have come in while we were stalking up the other side of Puddy Tat Hill, for now, instead of twenty geese, there were three times that number, a long melting line which dwindled, baying and crying, until we lost them against the grey loom of the hills.

15. *Away From it All*

THOSE moments when we can escape from the daily grind of business and its worries are perhaps the happiest in our brief existence.

Some who are born to greatness and who have perhaps to carry weighty affairs of state have found great solace in these days of freedom. One of the Chamberlains (I forget which) found rest and joy in the study of butterflies, and roamed the lovely forest of Wyre in quest of them. Another found solace in fishing; indeed in that art there is peace abounding, whether it is by rushing mountain river amidst the hills, with the sound of the becking grouse and curlew's call, or beside some lush Hampshire carrier where the huge trout stir as the light dies on the stream. Of all peaceful occupations fishing has most to recommend it, yet many find that they must have some measure of movement and excite-ment. Here the gun fills the need.

Most of my happiest moments 'away from it all' have been spent north of the Border, sometimes with rod but most often with the gun. You know, if you think a moment, it is not often one can enjoy a *really* happy holiday. If one is a family man, then the sea is universally voted the only place. And very nice it is. I would be the last to deny the pleasures of a summer sea and sands. Yet, most of us who are sportsmen may think within ourselves (never breathing a word of course to our wives), "Is this *really* the most enjoyable kind of holiday?" The answer will be "No", you know it is not. Be honest with yourself. And remember that "it's later than we think", the years are short, woefully so. For heaven's sake, sportsmen all, let everything and everyone go hang once in a while; worry, work, yes, and even family! I am not ashamed to say it. Let us, for a brief day or so, be boys again and recapture some of that old fire and enthusiasm, that very joy of life we once knew, that 'beginning of the holidays' feeling when the future is spread out rosily before us. Let us for a space forget such things as regular meals and wiping our boots when we come into the house! Once every year a man must assert himself, and we shall leave even our ladies behind, bless their hearts.

No woman born can understand this love of a man for the rod and the gun, and the quiet solitude of the hills and glens. When we are wildfowling or deer-stalking, we want no rustling of petticoats, no fragrant lures of womankind. This is a sterner time. We do not desire a smart hotel with bridge in the lounge at night, bobbing up to open doors, and empty talk of little things.

A flickering oil lamp, a pint of good ale perhaps, even a good wine—why not?—and above all things a roaring fire when the day is done—these things suffice. And I would add, let there be a friend or two so that you may gossip over the day's doings. The life of the hunting-lodge without the women, that is my ideal, that is the perfect background to shooting in the wild places.

But the usual run of men, myself included, have no hunting-lodge. The village inn, the crofter's cottage, must suffice. Good fowling quarters are very hard to find. For very many years I stayed with a dear old soul who owned the village stores in a certain Highland village. I had a large room in addition to a bed-room. Fires were generous, so was the food, and she used to cook for us mighty pies filled with curlew, redshank, green plover, and (sometimes) a duck or a moorhen thrown in—a real game pie, or *oystercock* pie, in fowler's parlance.

There are one or two pubs I know of where good quarters may be had, genuine fowlers' inns where one can get lunch or breakfast, dinner, or even tea, within half an hour of your coming. No word about dirty dogs or boots. You can throw your gear anywhere. I have even known a dead goose to be tossed on the bed! And the dog can curl up on the horse-hair sofa.

I remember a big hotel in the north where I once stayed, which was a place of horror. It was very large, very ornate, very cold and empty (it was out of the 'season'), and, I suspect, highly immoral.

The maids were blowsy and pimply, and the receptionist worse. What went on into the small hours was just nobody's business, for the ladies of this establishment nightly entertained their men friends. Their reception-room was just under my bedroom. Wild sexual orgies seemed to be going on.

We sought other rooms away from the town, but the fowling was poor and we soon went elsewhere.

There is a great gamble in trying new ground, yet if one does not move around one tends to overshoot a place; even a large estuary will not hold very many guns if they are after the fowl all the time.

On such a holiday, no time is lost; even the 'sawbath', when shooting is taboo, is not wasted, for then one may scout for feeding fowl in preparation for the next day. Many of these 'sawbath' scouting trips are remembered, and none more vividly than one bright, glittering day when Mac, Tony, and I made a long journey by car to seek out the geese. Even on the low ground the roads were treacherous; up on the high passes they were sheets of glass and the snow lay deep beside the way. There was no single cloud in the hard, blue sky, every loch and lochan was frozen from bank to bank. Blue sky above, blue shadows on the snow, black fir woods which seemed as cosy as rooms, for beneath the close-crowding stems the dead bracken, thinly powdered here and there with snow, glowed with rich, warm colour. Only the wayside burns still chattered gaily, winking and flashing in the brilliant sun. Such a scene might be anywhere in the Swiss Alps.

By and by the road dipped down and, after some hair-raising skids, we found ourselves among woods of beech, and then, breath-taking in its beauty, an old stone, ivy-clad bridge with high-flung arches which spanned a brawling river. A few hundred yards below the bridge on the far bank, a mass of wildfowl rested on a bright green bank. The sun had melted the snow at that spot, and maybe the warm bellies of the resting fowl had helped to thaw the white coverlet. The birds were wigeon, half a hundred birds, the cocks brilliant in the sunlight with their rose-pink heads and sulphur forehead caste marks. Even the sober plumaged ducks were colourful against that radiant background.

Most were asleep, but some were grazing whilst others swam in the open water close by, splashing and playing happily. Two curlew stalked about in the shallow by the bridge. All seemed as tame as fowl in a London park.

A few miles on we turned left by a wall of clipped beech, the highest beech hedge in Britain and justly famed for its unique beauty. Soon after, we came to a series of lochs beside the road, with dark fir woods mantling the opposite shores.

Here there was no open water, but each loch had its complement of fowl, a dark mass huddled motionless far out in the centre, looking like a rug laid down on the ice. The third loch was the largest, and near the far bank there was a strip of open water. In that strip no less than a hundred or so pinkfooted geese were gambolling and playing, whilst beyond, where the ground rose steeply to the foothills, was a vast field of stubble half-covered with snow. Upon this field geese were also feeding busily, three or four hundred, scattered all over the field like rooks.

Other small parties flew around and, as we watched this scene, enthralled, another bunch came winging over the snow-capped mountains to the south, to wheel, cackling musically, to join those on the field below them. It was a sight which can never be forgotten, and for a full hour we watched them through the telescope, their faint cries coming to us from across the frozen plain.

Mallard and a great number of wigeon were swimming about in the open strip of water near the bank, and three whooper swans swam there also, dwarfing the duck, their long, white necks rigid as pokers. Through the glass, the beautiful, clear, canary-yellow of their bills was distinctly visible and the elongated flat heads, almost reptilian in appearance, could be clearly seen.

Whoopers are common on most of the larger Highland lochs in the winter and are not unduly wild. I have sometimes seen them within a hundred yards of a main road bordering a loch. But they will not allow a close approach on foot and will swim away before you get within gun-shot range.

After a while all the geese feeding on the stubble began to troop down to the strip of open water, so that soon it was packed with wildfowl. They swam about preening and playing, dashing the sparkling drops over themselves, chasing each other, and making the spray fly in all directions.

They knew they were safe there and free from molestation, for I believe that this chain of lochs is seldom, if ever, shot during the season. The wild geese and ducks also resort to these havens all through the months of winter until prolonged frost locks all the open water. On this particular loch the ice was very thick, but the fowl had kept a channel open. As long as they frequented the place in such numbers, it would take very severe weather indeed to freeze it over entirely.

After the shooting season ends on the 31st of January, the geese become very tame. They have a full eight weeks of rest and they can fly back and forth to the coast without any volleys from the hidden dykes. This is an excellent thing. They leave these islands with no hard feelings, and so they return again in ever increasing numbers.

When I first began to take an interest in wildfowling, the season ended on the last day of February, and indeed February was about the best month of the whole winter for shooting wild geese.

Fresh arrivals keep coming from Northern Europe and there are perhaps more geese in Britain in February than in any other of the winter months. This especially applies to brent geese. Very few are seen at Holy Island before Christmas and the large lots do not come in until after January, unless the weather in Northern Europe is very severe.

I have never shot a brent goose as I am not a puntsman and the black geese are the puntsman's finest sea game. Only very rarely does it fall to the shore shooter to shoot a brent, but no fewer than sixteen were bagged with a shoulder gun at Holy Island on the 13th February, 1922. In January 1941, Group Captain Stratton shot eleven brent with a right and left at Thorney Island, Hampshire. He was using BB shot. I would rather shoot a brent than a barnacle, for they always seem to me to be a great prize.

They are small geese but very 'tubby', and I believe are excellent eating. Their heads are very distinctive, unlike those of any other wild geese. As in the whooper swan, they are elongated and flat, due to their mode of feeding, for the brent finds all its food on the ooze and eats the same sea grass as the wigeon.

I always feel uncomfortable when I shoot a barnacle, for one associates them with parks and ornamental lakes. And indeed this little pied goose (some barnacles are little bigger than a large mallard) is very decorative.

But the prize of all the geese is the greylag, ancestor of our farm-yard goose. He is a real 'goosey' looking goose with something of the latter's same ponderous rolling gait, and he is vastly superior to his domesticated relative on the table.

One winter I tried the Beauly Firth, for I had talked with a man

116

who had shot there and found it an excellent locality. But on the firth there are no marshes in the proper sense. There are flat goose fields inshore, a sea-wall, and mud flats, typical of many of the Highland firths.

I went in January, and the weather was open. Very few geese were to be seen, and all the time I was there I only saw a party of about 200, which kept far out in the firth and never seemed to flight in at dawn or dusk.

There was good wigeon flighting on the flooded fields behind the sea-wall, but the moon was wrong for me and, though they came in as thick as bees after sunset, it was too dark to see to shoot. The only thing I remember about that trip was a fine golden eagle wheeling over a splintered fir near Dalwhinnie and a stag and his hinds on the very top of a snow-capped mountain. I had a powerful glass and could see him clearly, pawing at the snow to get at the heather, whilst all around his hinds were lying down like cows in a field. The old stag would never feed for long, but raised his head and stared about him for minutes on end. All around him was a snowy waste, peak after snow-clad peak, stretching away northwards against the drab and bitter sky. It was a sight which made even the fruitless trip to Beauly worth while.

16. Little Longlegs

IT has long been debated what is fair game for the wildfowler. Some express horror at shooting curlew, knot, redshank, dunlin, and green plover.

All these birds are, however, legitimate game, with the exception of green plover, which is now on the protected list. There is no doubt that the green plover has become scarce of late years, and increased mechanization is perhaps to blame for this. Like the corncrake, it flourished in the days of the horse-drawn plough, but the advent of the tractor has meant that many eggs are annually destroyed. The green plover, by the way, is a very sporting bird and extremely good upon the table.

The test of what is fair game can be summed up in the word 'edibility'. No bird should ever be shot unless it is edible. Green plover are certainly in the latter category and I prefer them to snipe.

In the past we have had some very good sport with plover on the evening flight. They come in very late from the fields and are invariably in range, though by no means easy to shoot. They twist and jig as they come over the sea-wall, and moreover they soon get to know how to look after themselves when they have been shot at.

Curlews are always fair game. They are excellent if cooked

correctly and hung for a few days before eating. Their habits are perhaps more fixed than those of any other wildfowl. They have their own flight lines which they follow day after day, and they keep to the same section of marsh.

In this respect they remind me of a certain butterfly, the marbled white, which keeps to its own territory, governed in its case by the food plant. They may always be found in a certain restricted area in comparative abundance, yet other ground adjoining, which to our eyes is exactly similar, is always avoided.

The curlew is a wary bird and has very sharp sight. Its time of flight, unlike that of the geese and duck, is governed entirely by the tide. Once you have found the line of flight on an estuary, you have only to be there at certain set times and you are sure of a shot or two.

When the sea begins to cover the muds the curlews retreat before it, along with the redshanks, knot, and dunlin. They feed a few feet before the advancing water and, when within two hundred yards or so of the shore, they lift in little bunches and go inland to feed on the grass pastures.

During high water most of the curlews will be inland, some-times at a considerable distance from the sea. There they feed along with green plover, starlings, and rooks, but as soon as the tide withdraws from high-sea mark they begin to dribble back, following it out in the reverse direction.

Sometimes there will be a small area of marsh which, on a moderate tide, is surrounded by water, and they will often retreat to this as the sea comes in until they are packed so close that they can hardly move or stretch a leg. I have in mind one such place on a northern estuary which is always thick with curlews at high water and they are well content to rest there, waiting for the ebb, sleeping and preening.

I have lain in ambush of this little marsh, within a few yards of it, and have seen them come in in little trips of three and four birds until the whole area in front of me has been a mass of brown-striated backs. I have got into position an hour before high water and have seen far out on the tide the tiny, black figures busily moving about, drawing ever nearer as the tide crept onward, until with a musical yodelling the big bunches came to drop down among those already among the coarse tussocks of rush.

Lying close to a big flock of curlews is a most interesting experience, as many a bird watcher in his hide has found. They have a musical duck-like chatter which is a sound of contentment, not unlike the buzz made by a big flock of barnacle geese when heard at close quarters.

Though curlews feed at night under the moon, they are primarily day feeders, and in this respect they differ from the geese.

The little dumpy knot, that delightful little wader of the tide-line, is a great favourite of mine. It is a local bird, I find, and in some estuaries is entirely absent. I have found it in great abundance on the Northumberland coast, notably in the vicinity of Holy Island, and on the Essex marshes. Of all the tide-line birds it is the most delicious on the table. It is perhaps the best eating of all wildfowl with the exception of teal. I would not class it as a very sporting bird, as one can rarely get flighting shots. But a hide on the tide edge will sometimes provide good sport, especially at high water, when the big flocks, curling like silver smoke, pass along high-sea mark.

Golden plover are very sporting birds and well worthy of the fowler's attentions. They flight well in certain localities. They seem to feed more ashore than on the muds and, like the curlew, may be shot on the flood as they come over the sea-wall. It is a common bird in winter on the Solway, and there one may some-times see vast flocks feeding on the inland grass fields.

The best golden plover shooting is to be had in the autumn, and this especially applies to the Solway. Along parts of that coast the merse edge provides excellent hides. Great slabs of peaty earth have broken away from the mainland, forming wonderful hiding-places. You are sheltered from the cold winds, and there you can sit as in a cosy room and from your windows command a wide view of the sea. In September and October, especially in the early evenings, the golden plover come in from the fields and they will also follow along the edge of the tide, often within range of your ambush. When they settle on the stony foreshore, it is amazing how their mottled, golden-brown plumage blends with their surroundings and they are almost as difficult to see as snipe.

Dunlin I never shoot, though they may be considered fair game. They are not good sporting birds, however, and not at all appetizing on the table, as their flesh has an oily taste.

The same applies to oyster-catchers and shelduck, both species should be off the fowler's list. Some gunners shoot 'oysters' and profess to like their taste, but I have never found them palatable, and they are rather stupid little birds, not very sharp-sighted, and sometimes very trusting. On moonlight nights when the tide floods, they rise in vast clouds from the sea's edge and fly hither and thither piping hysterically, a plaintive, petulant pipe. They come low over your hide in a great mass like a wigeon pack, and the shore popper (the Cockney Tailor of Colonel Hawker) ups with his gun and has both barrels into the flock, littering the marsh with broken, pied beauties. For the oyster-catchers are absurdly marked: they remind me of painted wooden birds (and their stance is wooden also), black and white with little blending of the two, scarlet bill, high forehead, great round eye, and orange legs.

In the same category is the shelduck, again a brilliantly-patterned bird, black, white, and wonderful russet umbers and kingly scarlet-knobbed beak. I always feel his proper place is not on the wild tide but in a London park. Because of his pied plumage, which is visible over the mud flats for a mile or more, this unhappy duck is not like other ducks (save the golden-eye, which sometimes nests in burrows), for he has to conceal his nest in a rabbit-hole in the dunes. That is why it is found on coasts where sand-dunes abound, such as in Norfolk. Again, some 'pipit poppers' shoot these gaudy creatures, but they are quite inedible.

As a general rule, with me at any rate, all the little 'longlegs' of the coast pass me by unharmed. I prefer watching to eating them. To see those moving silvery puffs of fairylike smoke passing along the far tide-line is one of the sights which warm the fowler's heart.

One last word about one other 'little longlegs'—the redshank. I must confess that redshank shooting is quite delightful. On the Norfolk marshes you may walk the dykes and drains and have a really good day's sport at 'shank. They are very sporting birds and quite difficult to hit, as they travel with great swiftness, jinking as they go. There is another point in their favour: they are nearly always on the move, flickering from dyke to dyke or, when the tide is flooding, moving in swiftly-turning companies across the marsh.

They have very sharp sight, perhaps more so than any other of the waders, and their shrill whistles are one of the sounds of that land between the tides. For some reason, I think the redshank is not so common as it used to be, though I can think of no explanation of its scarcity in some localities where it was once so plentiful.

It is the 'little longlegs' of the coast which beguile many a long wait which otherwise might be dull and irksome. One never tires of watching these little people going about their business, whether it is under the moon or at high noonday.

The tide-line is their world, a world which is governed by the tides. Sleeping and eating depend on the movement of the sea, and the time they like best of all is when at last the grey waters slip silkily back along the gutters and a fresh harvest is exposed; it is then they can have, with the curlews, the major banquet of the day.

scaup alighting

17. *One Morning Flight*

WHAT are the first birds to move on morning flight?
This, of course, varies from coast to coast, but I have
noticed that it is rarely the geese; indeed geese are
usually the last to leave the sea for their feeding grounds inland.

Let us for a moment visit a Scottish firth I know very well, and
which I have seen under all conditions, in frosty, hard weather, in
driving snow, and on those calm, mild mornings we so often get
on the western seaboard. Let us take for example one of these
'open' mornings in early January.

There has been the usual procedure so well known to fowlers:
the shrill of the alarm-clock, the reluctant rising from bed (and it is
amazing how the body complains at having to rouse itself at
5.30 a.m. on a winter's morning), the quick gulp of hot tea, and a
sandwich, and the journey to the shore.

All this takes place in darkness, for on this morning we have
chosen there is no moon. It is at such periods the flight is most
sustained. When the moon is full, wildfowl feed largely at night.

We have groped our way over the fields, we have reached the
sea-wall, and before us, showing as an indistinct blur, is the open
sea and the dark tones of the marsh.

We know the route well, even on so dark a morning, and are not
trapped by that hidden gutter, or the soft spot which is so beloved

by snipe. Actually, we disturb one as we pass this little bog, though it is, of course, invisible. It gives one *scaape* and we hear the 'prutt' of its spring into the air.

As always on the coast, there is a wind, though this will die at dawn. Twenty minutes creek-jumping and we reach our favourite place, an angle of the creek where the mud forms a seat. In front there is a low parapet, exactly like a trench of that other war which is now only dimly remembered.

There is no sound of geese, not a croak, not a call—no sound at all save the far-off murmur of the tide.

Slowly the light grows over the sea, and then strange, dusky shapes appear out of the dimness. They may be flotsam of the tide-line, they may be tussocks, they may be geese—the eye strains to make them out.

A curlew calls far away over the flats; you can hear it passing down the tide, its voice growing fainter. Curlews are ever restless birds, even on the darkest night.

There is always this wait, but how enjoyable it is! Never a dull moment! The dog beside you, crouched low in the crab-grass, has his head up, staring out towards the sea. He hears and smells things you are not aware of; his frame quivers against you, for he is excited. A comfort, too, on a cold morning; a dog is a hot-water bottle as well as a retriever of his master's game.

Now the sea is visible, a spear of brightness, and yet the dark, mysterious lumps are still unrecognizable. Funny how easy it is to imagine they are moving! If you look at them long enough you can swear they take the forms of geese, and you can even see their spindly necks and small, wise heads.

Whistling wings pass over, not from the sea, but from the land. A big party of duck have passed directly over you, but you could not see them, though the dog did. He stares up and takes a sidelong glance at you which is very amusing.

After the duck comes another party, you saw those for an

instant and they were in range. The gun twitches on the arm and is couched again; no gunner in all the world could have taken so fleeting a shot.

A goose calls afar off, another answers, and then there comes the thin keening of gulls, a cold; thin-drawn sound which always seems to me to have something of the desolation of the vast seas in it. And then the first birds come. They are gulls, a small party, wagging their way inland in a compact bunch as orderly as geese. Silently they pass. Soon after, come others, until wherever you look, gulls are coming in.

Then a bunch of curlews. These, unlike the gulls who came silently, call to one another—clear yodelling cries, sounds beloved to the fowler; their wings are working at twice the pace of the gulls'.

Those dark lumps out there are tussocks: at least you think so. They have not moved. Your imagination has played another trick. A redshank appears suddenly, sees you and gives a *twee* of alarm. Immediately afterwards a mallard plumps down on the wet sand not thirty yards off. This so often happens at morning flight. No doubt he has been feeding inland and has stopped for a snack before passing on to the sea. The spaniel's ears nearly fall off, and you whisper to him to keep down. But before you can begin to lift the gun, the mallard has seen you and is up. By the time the gun is at the shoulder, he is away.

All this has taken a second or two. When you next look at the 'tussocks' your heart gives a bound. They are not tussocks, but sleeping geese! They sit all along the fringe of the marsh-edge, strung out like beads on a string. Every bird has its head tucked in, but you can do nothing about it. They look just in range, which means they are over a hundred yards away, and even as you look one pulls out its head and stands up. These geese have no doubt but lately come in, and are off their guard. One by one they wake up. They are still silent; geese resting on the marsh-edge are often as quiet as mice.

Now the birds begin to waddle slowly away. They sway, or rather roll, as they walk, like sailors—a true nautical gait. It is difficult to judge distance and movement on the open ooze. You cannot tell for a moment whether they are going away from you or walking in, but you know it cannot be the latter, as geese never walk inshore at dawn. Every bird—there must be thirty or more in front of you—is swaying but all are dwindling in size.

Then, with a clamour, and a threshing of wings, all are up. No, they didn't see you. They are eager for a wash and brush-up in the fresh burn-water which flows in over the muds half a mile from shore. The whole line swings right-handed, and you see them land again, far out on the burn-edge, where they begin to splash and cackle and chase each other. Not until the sun peeps over the mountains, and the whole firth is visible in the clear pellucid light, do the geese start to think about breakfast.

There are fully three hundred pinks and greys far out on the sand-banks, arranged in a black ribbon. One end of the ribbon lifts and the ripple passes like a snake along the length. A moment's pause and the full glorious music crashes out as though at the bidding of a conductor's baton. Now, as you look, to left, to right, the limpid dawn sky is spotted with weaving bunches, all passing inland. What a moment that is! If you see no drama in this, then you are no fowler.

Most parties are low when they cross the muds, but they are climbing all the time, and as they cross the gullies they are out of gun-shot. Some fool along the coast has two barrels. You see a skein lift, and a moment later hear the shots—a tiny double pop. One big V comes straight for your ambush. Out of range, don't be a fool! Yet the urge to fire is almost irresistible as with wry neck you look upwards under the rim of your hat. Clear in the light they pass right over, each stern snowy white, with paddles neatly tucked, necks nodding, all cackling. Some writers call it 'honking'. No goose honks save the Canada goose, which makes a noise like a deep-toned cow-bell.

We might as well face it: we are not going to get a shot this morning. We need wind, the answer to the fowler's prayer, to keep them down.

And then happens one of those quite unforeseen happenings which add so much to the uncertain joys of fowling. The sun well up, and the flight over, we are tramping back across the marsh, thinking of breakfast, as hungry as those old grey-bellies which are now lowering on some distant pasture. There is a single croak behind us. We swing round, dropping by instinct to one knee. And there, almost on us, is a party of six greys intent on committing suicide! Why this sometimes happens, I have no idea, unless the geese are watching that other shore-popper who is making his painful stumbling way to shore half a mile to our left.

The gun goes up, the geese scatter at the movement, each bird climbing desperately, silently, not even calling, so intent are they on gaining height. Bang! and again bang! The contents of the long cases of BB shot whistle skywards. The cackling breaks out and you cannot believe your eyes when no goose drops. Are these birds wearing armoured waistcoats? You've bungled a good chance.

Unbelieving, sick with anger and disappointment, you stand like a heron there on the saltings, fingers automatically reloading. You watch them reform and go on steadily shorewards. They are over the sea-wall now. Quite suddenly, without any fuss or warning, you see a goose slump from the middle of the skein. One moment it was flying as well as the others; now it is falling like a black rag to earth. Fortune has relented at the last moment. You have a goose down after all.

You arrive at the bank in record time, with your spaniel bounding in front. You range the sea-wall frantically, straining to catch a glimpse of an inert grey form. But the wind stirs the grass, other geese pass in unheeded (they are still moving in), a hare sits up in the middle of a green field washing its paws. You rake the pastures with your glasses. Farm-carts move towards steaming middens, fieldfares cluck overhead, all the bustle of the day has begun. The spaniel ranges along the foot of the sea-wall his tail wagging urgently. Did that goose drop this side of the bank or over the land? How difficult it is to tell from the marsh!

Then comes the supreme moment. The dog pauses and casts quickly. He stops half-hidden by the rushes; his head is down, there is a pause, then he raises it—and, yes! There in his mouth is a bulky, grey form, limp, with wings drooped awry.

"Good old fellow; good old chap; bring him on; bring him on!" Is there any prize so much worth while as this massive, grey bird, warm to the touch, with hanging, pink paddles, and stern as white as sea foam?

There is a point in this account which is worth remembering. Always watch the skeins after you have fired, follow them out of sight. One single BB shot may have gone home without your knowledge, and many a bird is lost in this way. The pattern of BB at long range is fairly open; it is often the single pellet which brings down a bird.

18. "Up the Burn"

SNOW—glittering, crisp, and thin. Frost—locking every
flash and runnel save the burn which still flowed dark and
swift between daggers of ice. Sun—shining from a cloudless
sky and the dazzle from this white world trying to the eyes.

Such were the conditions one January morning when Mac,
Tony, and I drove slowly along, scanning for geese. Morning after
morning, the flight on the shore had been fruitless, for the hard
weather had skimmed the firth of fowl. An odd greylag or two
going in against the rosy-dawn light, that was all, and the chances
of connecting on that long coast-line were thousands to one. Yet I
had enjoyed those mornings. The sugary ice rustled when you
tramped out to flight, one's breath froze on moustaches, fingers
ached with cold, you could barely touch the naked gun-barrels—
they almost seemed to sear the hand.

We drove along at about ten miles an hour, pulling up now and
then to rake the goose grounds with our glasses. Hares, partridges,
pheasants, rooks, lapwings, and gulls, that is all we saw.

Back into the warmth of the shooting-brake again; slide,
wag, of our back wheels as we started. So it went on all that
morning.

And then, at one of these halts, the swinging stalking-glass came
to a steady point. Seven greylags sat under a thorn-tree on the
banks of a little burn. The burn was eight feet below the level of

the fields, by walking a few yards through a chicken-run behind the grieve's cottage we could be in it. It was a piece of cake!

These seven birds, the only geese we had seen in two days, seemed heaven-sent. There they were, all sitting down under the little may-tree as comfortable and cheeky as you please, like farm-yard geese!

We drew up the van in the shadow of the grieve's house and tossed for who was to try a stalk. The two losers could do nothing but sit in the van and watch developments, for to try to post a gun to intercept the geese on their way to the sea would be unwise, for the birds could command all the flat land for miles.

Tony won the toss, and climbed over the wire fence into the chicken-run. Doubling low, he gained the bank of the burn, and the last thing we saw was his head sliding from view. The burn was wadable, though the water came to the tops of Tony's waders. There was nothing to do but wait. We estimated twenty minutes for the stalk, and if nothing untoward happened at least one of those greys was as good as in the bag.

Under that may-tree there was a little green grass, for the field sloped a little facing south—the only green patch for miles probably. That is why the geese had gone there.

The minutes passed. In the fowl-run the hens clucked and moved around, starlings whistled, a distant tractor tuttered.

Half an hour passed, and still the geese remained under the may-tree. Three-quarters of an hour. What had happened? Tony must surely be well up by now. Had he become bogged in the burn?

I watched the geese through the glass. Six of the greys were still sitting down. The seventh was up and stalking to and fro, grazing. Every now and then he lifted his long neck and made a steady scrutiny of his surroundings.

Then he said something to the others and they all stood up, staring at the burn. "Any moment now," whispered Mac. "Wait for it!"

But we continued to wait and the geese all began to walk slowly away into the field. Ten yards, twenty . . . soon they were well beyond gun-shot of the burn and at last, with a cackle, they were up.

Slowly gaining height they turned towards the hills, and for quite five minutes we watched them through the glass, dwindling until they were lost.

There was a commotion in the hen-run and Tony's head appeared over the bank, and we heard his report. All had gone well for the first one hundred yards, and then he found the burn took a left-hand crook. Those geese under the thorn-tree could command the last one hundred yards of the burn, they could look along its complete length and that was why Tony had been unable to gain another yard. They hadn't been so foolish as they seemed!

There was nothing then but to go home to lunch. We had been up since dawn and were mighty hungry, and no more geese were in sight. It looked like another blank day.

At 2 p.m. we were back by the grieve's house—a forlorn hope. But in our absence a pack of pinks had come in: about thirty birds. They were not in the 'may-tree' field, however, but had pitched on a field of winter wheat over the burn, but within two hundred yards of the same may-tree.

They were unapproachable; many had their heads up, and it looked at first a hopeless venture. Then Mac nobly volunteered to try a drive. Tony and I got down into the burn (again by way of the chicken-run), and Mac turned the van round and drove half a mile back along the road, leaving the vehicle by a telegraph post.

I had no confidence in this drive. Geese of all birds are the most uncertain, and you never know which way they will 'go out' from their feeding field. The only thing you can be certain of is that they will rise into the wind. But that afternoon there was no wind and the sun still shone on the glittering snow. How large those geese appeared in the centre of the wheat: as big as turkeys!

We made quick work of our stalk up the burn for the banks were ample and we could walk along the muddy bed of the stream. The only thing we had to be careful of was the floating ice, and here and there the water was covered over with thin sheets of it.

I reached my fancied spot, thirty yards short of the may-tree, and Tony went fifty yards beyond it. Then we lay down on the bank.

Through the drifted snow (and it was quite deep on the bank) the dun withered grass protruded. On the bank-top it formed quite a fringe, though I dare not look over, for the geese were not more than one hundred yards out on the wheat.

Again the well-known wait and speculations as to what Mac was doing. There was no sound from the field and I almost thought the geese must have lifted. Then one solitary pink called 'quink wink' and I knew that they were still there. At that sound I slipped the catch from safe, and my heart began to beat a little faster.

Still the minutes passed. A handsome fieldfare came dipping to the thorn-tree and there he sat bolt upright, bill tilted upwards, turning his head from side to side. He did not see me in the burn and began to pluck the few remaining berries, clucking with satisfaction.

Then there came a muffled roar of wings and a burst of goose music. They were up!

I dare not lift my head. I lay pressed against the cold snow, my heart beating fast.

Through the fringe of dead grass I saw the ragged, black mob heading straight for Tony. On they came and then swung round —then they were coming straight for me. I was looking at the whole skein head on.

Another fifty yards and they would be slap over me, but the leader turned well out and headed for the sea.

The birds were flying in a V-formation and the nearest bird of the leg looked a possible shot. I fired with BB shot, and he turned over and hit the snow.

It is always a great triumph to bring off a drive like this, and it was with a tremendous sense of satisfaction that I lifted my prize by his pink paddles. What a lovely bird he was: spotless, un-smeared by mud, not even a crimson stain to mark where my single BB shot had reached a vital spot.

19. *An Autumn Goose Hunt*

THE hen wives of Bowes Moor were putting their charges to bed as we crossed the Pennines one gloomy November afternoon.

Over Kaber Fell and Barras the autumn dusk was deepening to night and against the pale, rain-washed western sky a massive black cloud, shaped like a giant's head, reared fantastically over the darkening fells. Here and there by lonely farms white troops of ducks and geese were waddling homewards in single file after a jolly day in the neighbouring burns.

We climbed higher towards the summit, past the solitary ale-house where once Colonel Hawker stayed and where he shot his first grouse with 'Kitty Lockey for pilot'.

I remembered how, on the 29th of October, 139 years before (almost to the day), he made the following entry in his famous diaries:

"The weather having suddenly changed to a very hard frost with sharp winds, I, after getting some breakfast, started with my dog, and Kitty Lockey for pilot. Within 250 yards of the ale house, Nero found three grouse, then two and seven more.

(I looked at my watch, and found that we had seen these six brace within nine minutes from leaving the door.) Within 25 minutes of our throwing off we found two packs of about ten and twelve each; and, in short, saw about 40 brace during our walk, all within one mile; and two thirds of them within less than half a mile from the public house! And some close to the road, where the mail and other coaches pass!"

Hawker managed to get his grouse later that morning and it took him a deal of trouble. But it was his first and he was in triumphant mood.

In his day, anyone could shoot over Bowes Moor, for it was before the days of grouse preserves, and a journey to the Highlands from Hawker's home at Longparish in Hampshire was a terrific undertaking and took considerably longer than travelling to France.

Mac, Charles, and I were travelling north for the first time in autumn. I wished to test the stories I had heard of the grey legions of geese which were but newly in in early November; moreover, I had never seen my beloved Highland firths in their late autumn guise.

The day was typical of the season, lowering and with bursts of rain. The sombre fells were magnificent in their rich colours, madders, ochres, lion-tinted moor grass which climbed away to the horizons all around us. Here and there lights twinkled from the solitary farms, each with its group of plane-trees and branching sycamores planted on the northern side. And very soon, in pouring rain and darkness, we saw the glittering lights of Carlisle; and journey's end was almost in sight.

We stayed that night at a little fishing inn on the banks of the Esk and dined regally on shrimp cocktail and roast pheasants, with a very fine Burgundy to accompany our feast. This last was a piece of extravagance, but the occasion warranted it and we were about to say good-bye to civilization.

Next day we were again on the road up the glorious valley of the Esk. The beeches clothing the steep riverside hills were beyond all description in their autumn flames (when we returned that way ten days later every tree was bare), but the Esk was below summer level owing to the dry October.

It was late afternoon on the following day when we arrived in the land beloved. As soon as we reached the goose grounds near the firth, glasses were out, and now and again we stopped to scan the favourite fields. But no signs of geese were visible, not a single one, either in the air or on the ground.

This was disturbing. Not one of us said anything, but for my part I began to wonder what we should do if the geese had *not* arrived. It had been a long journey and things did not look promising.

As evening drew on we went ~~direct~~ to the shore, and it was there (at 4 p.m.) Mac spotted the first skein of geese heading in for the firth about a mile distant. It was a bundle of about fifty pinks and they were flying low in the teeth of the rising wind. Actually, until we disembarked on the sea-bank, we had not realized how hard it was blowing, and that night and the next day were destined to be the wildest in Scotland for many years, a perfect godsend to the wildfowler who always prays for wind.

The tide was flooding full, tawny ochre-green, slashed with white foam. We sought the shelter of two peat-stacks, and behind these we crouched, glad indeed to find some shelter from the gale.

And then unfolded one of the most dramatic flights I have ever witnessed on this particular coast. At 4.20 p.m. the geese began to stream into the firth. I am reasonably sure that they were all new arrivals and we were witnessing a thing I had always wanted to see: the arrival of the geese from their arctic homes.

In the short space of twenty minutes we must have seen close on 2,000 pinkfeet arrive. They came in from the north over the mountains, skein after skein, as far as the eye could see.

Some of the skeins passed directly over us as we crouched behind the peat-stacks, most were within easy shot. The wind was so strong that the sound of their voices was lost on the gale. All up that stretch of coast bordering the firth we could see them coming. Some were in small family parties, but most were in big skeins, dim, weaving lines and clots against the dreary November dusk.

There was little sleep for me that night, and when I did drop off it was to dream of geese. As I lay awake I could hear the wind still raving, and wondered whether it could possibly hold until dawn.

Long before it was light, we were up and away and in position before any fowl began to move. But what an effort it was to trudge across the marsh against that gale! Perhaps I was unfit after weeks of sedentary life, perhaps it was excitement, but by the time I reached my favourite creek my heart was behaving queerly.

Charles had gone off to the right, Mac had disappeared into the darkness to the east, and so wild was the wind I never heard them shooting, even when the 'flight of flights' began.

When I reached my creek I found it untenable. The tide was flooding full and even the tall reeds were awash. So I had to be content with staying under cover of the high reeds and trust to fate to send the birds over me.

They began to move early: fieldfares first, clucking close at hand in the big reed beds where they had passed the night; then mallard, beating in head-high all round me. I have never seen so many mallard on this coast before and every one that passed me was very low. Yet I was after the geese, so had to let them go, and in any case I only had one's and BB's in my Magnum.

At about 7.50 a.m. the pinks began to come, and for the next half-hour I witnessed an amazing flight.

They, like the ducks, were low and most were in easy range, but the shooting was most difficult in the gale, for besides the wind it was raining hard. One pinkfoot fell out in front where the creeks were awash, and when I tried to reach it I found it an impossible task. Only when the light had come and the tide had turned did I seek it and found it lying floating in a marsh pool, belly up.

Another goose I dropped on the path behind me, neatly done, for if it had fallen into the high reeds I might never have found it. Another, a single bird coming up the marshes from behind, was hard hit with BB. It tried to turn and reach the firth, but the wind took it and whirled it over the sea-wall. I watched it as it topped the trees, and then saw it collapse and fall. When I found it it was lying dead on the open grass field surrounded by astonished cattle.

Charles at Smith's Post had seven down and one lost; Mac with his eight-bore had three; I also had accounted for three. We should have shot double that number.

This particular flight is perhaps the best I have ever had. It so happened that tide and wind coincided with dawn flight, and the fact that the firth was full of geese newly in made it one of those rare occasions which happen but once or twice in the average wildfowler's lifetime.

20. The Lighter Vein

WILDFOWLERS are a strange race, quite apart from the average shooting man, as I have already said. I don't suppose the sport will ever become popular, for it is the roughest form of rough shooting. For so many, a day's shooting means keepers and beaters to drive your game and plan the attack, fixed stands from which to shoot, the minimum of walking, a big lunch at midday, and all the rest of it. I enjoy a day of this sort once in a while, but it cannot be compared to wildfowling where you have to work very hard to get a shot and occasionally undergo very great physical discomfort. I can't imagine many comfortable, old tweed-clad squires and colonels lying out in a wet ditch in pouring rain from dawn to midday on the chance of a shot. Yet the greater the effort, the more you have to endure in the way of physical discomfort, the more you appreciate your shot when it does come along. In all fairness to the aforesaid old squires and colonels, I must say that many I have known have confessed to me that a 'walk round' a rough shoot on a winter's day with a good dog is more to their taste than the planned and ordered drive. They are potential fowlers.

The fact is, of course, that wildfowling proper offers such unique advantages to anyone who is interested in wildfowl, apart from shooting them. The effect of dawn coming up over a lonely estuary is, in itself, a reward for early rising and cold fingers and toes. And what of that magic of the 'moon fields', as Peter Scott so aptly puts it, when the pinkfeet are flighting on a winter's night and you hear their unearthly music drawing near against the frosty stars! In this book I have tried to capture some of these memorable moments.

In midwinter, at the moonless periods, shooting ends at sun-down and there is the long wait until the following dawn. This time is spent gossiping round the fire, quaffing honest ale, and fighting one's battles over again. At such times it often amuses me to reflect on the humorous side of our sport.

There's no denying it that the wildfowler dressed for the fray is something of a figure of fun. The huge thigh boots, the balaclavas and deer-stalkers, the mufflers, the mittens, the outrageous tattered garments which make up his apparel make him look like a comic circus clown. Add to this the red, frostbitten noses and watering eyes . . . no wonder many think us slightly 'touched'.

On a wildfowling trip, though your actual shooting will nearly always be a solitary affair, it is very pleasant to have one or two companions interested in the same sport who can share their experiences with you. It is fun to compare notes after the flight is over.

Sitting in my solitary gutter at dawn, I wonder for instance how Charles is doing at Smith's Post or how the redoubtable Mac, with his 'mountain gun', is faring at his pet ambush on the tide edge a mile to the east of me. And when the full-flooding sun-light of a piping winter's morning tells you the flight is over and you make your way back to the bank, you will take a jealous scrutiny through the glasses at those other figures 'coming off'. Do their game bags bulge? Do they walk as if burdened with some-thing more than a gun? Is there the tell-tale black 'something' dangling from the right hand?

I think that there should be a list of penalties and rewards for good and bad behaviour on the marsh, and for my own amuse-ment I have made a list of what I call 'fines' and 'bonuses' for good and bad behaviour. I'm afraid that only those who have done much fowling will appreciate the finer points, but here is the scale

of fines and bonuses set out for my fellow fowlers, and it may
cause them a little amusement. Some are so subtle that the tyro
will fail to grasp their import, others are obvious. Anyway, here
they are:

1. Coming home early and first back at the car   FINE
2. Going to sleep in the middle of the day (even
   after a good lunch)   FINE
3. Going in over your wader tops at flight (usually
   by stepping into a hidden gutter)   FINE
4. Mistaking sheep, pheasants, telegraph wires,
   rooks, and curlews for feeding or flying geese   HEAVY FINE
5. A certain reluctance to undertake a wet and
   arduous stalk   HEAVY FINE
6. Failing to rise when the alarm-clock rings   HEAVY FINE
7. Going to sleep in the car when scouting for
   feeding geese on the fields   HEAVY FINE
8. Showing yourself too soon when geese are on
   the move   HEAVY FINE
9. Insufficient camouflage to your hide   HEAVY FINE
10. 'Cracking up', i.e. showing signs of illness,
    cold, rheumatism, lumbago, etc.   FINE
11. Reluctance to interview farmers for permission
    to shoot geese on their fields   FINE
12. Coming home late after 'flight' is obviously
    over. (This shows keenness on the part of the
    fowler so is treated as a minor offence)   SMALL FINE
13. Reluctance to go out 'Moonflighting' on a
    frosty night when the warmth of the fire and
    prospect of good ale forms a counter-attraction   HEAVY FINE
14. Snoring   FINE
15. Not cleaning gun before you clean yourself on
    return from flight   FINE
16. Missing an easy shot   HEAVY FINE

17. Not keeping a look-out *all round you* when geese are on the move   FINE
18. Standing about during flight with no cover   VERY HEAVY FINE
19. Too fond of the 'bar'   FINE
20. Shooting inedible wildfowl, including gulls   HEAVY FINE
21. Shooting at ducks when geese are in the vicinity   FINE
22. Dalliance with farmers' pretty daughters   FINE

Now for the bonuses.

23. Interviewing farmers with a view to obtaining permission to try for geese on their land   DOUBLE BONUS
24. Undertaking an arduous, wet and protracted stalk   BONUS
25. Right and left at flighting geese   DOUBLE BONUS
26. Identifying feeding geese   BONUS
27. A long stalk through the plickplack on a frosty morning (even if fruitless)   BONUS
28. General hardihood and fearlessness   BONUS

And so on and so on. Wildfowlers can make their own lists. All very childish, I suppose, but it does give cause for hilarity.

Anyone who has done a fortnight on the coast with two companions will be able to appreciate the finer points. Take, for instance, the first morning flight. There is no need for any alarm-clock, you and your companions have been awake most of the night, you are up and dressing before it rings. But by the fourth or fifth day each individual is more reluctant to rise from bed, and by the end of the time I have known keen fowlers shamelessly turn over and go to sleep again when the alarm goes off, thus incurring the heaviest of all possible fines!

It is not that one's enthusiasm has ebbed: it is usually sheer bodily fatigue. After a week's strenuous wildfowling, the prospect of the 'Sawbath' is a very welcome one. For once you can 'hog' on until 9 or 10 a.m., though any outward and visible exhibition of satisfaction incurs a heavy fine. So one has to be careful.

Asking farmers for permission is a thing I detest, but Mac, whenever he comes with me, tots up a formidable total of bonuses for this particular task. True, there was the time I have described when, at a certain farm, the door was opened by a lovely lady, and Mac disappeared inside the house and did not emerge for a considerable period of time (which both Tony and I considered unwarrantable). Hence Rule 22, which was hastily put to the committee and carried without a division that same evening, despite Mac's protestations.

Rule 4 (mistaken identity of feeding and flying geese) may seem strange to the non-fowling fraternity. But when one is suffering from an acute attack of goose fever even such things as distant telegraph wires can be mistaken for flying geese. I believe Peter Scott mentions this in *Morning Flight*. This malady plays tricks with one's sight.

I doubt whether any cure will be found for this distressing complaint of goose fever. Once the victim is infected with the bug (it is invariably caught from someone else, usually when one is young) he will suffer from it every year of his life until he is too senile to appreciate the full flavour of life's good things.

You may look for the first symptoms in October with the coming of the fieldfares. Restless nights full of goose dreams, 'moonfields', and celestial chimings are the main characteristics of this disease, this, and a certain wild look in the eye. Wildfowlers' wives ('goose widows') must be understanding at these periods.

By Christmas-time the fever is at its height. Once when I went north after the geese in early winter, before my goose fever had developed, I hoped to allay the malady. I made a bad mistake. The following January I had the worst attack ever, even though I had bagged my quota of geese.

But seriously, there is one interesting point here. Every autumn, at about the time the grey geese are coming to these shores from their arctic homes, I have a certain set dream, and it is a wonderful one. I find myself at a great height above the earth. Before me thin veils of cloud are drifting and very soon I see, far up, hidden now and again by those whisps of drifting vapour, the long arrow heads, the great travelling skeins, passing in majestic and silent array miles above the earth.

And again in the spring I have another dream, but this is very different. It is of sunlit green fields. The hedges are bursting into bud, birds are singing, the sky is blue, with white, puffy clouds drifting lazily over. And then into the picture the geese come, not flying high, but low and clear in the sunlight with every detail plain. They alight all down the slope of the green field where celandine and daisy make a coloured carpet. The geese are on their way north again, but this time in leisurely fashion, dallying by the way, odd and out of place in such a verdant, sunny background.

For years now I have had these dreams, and others have noted similar mental images.

21. *Geese on the Fields*

GOOSE-HUNTING inland is totally different from shooting on the shore. It is, as I have said elsewhere, not so enjoyable as the dawn or evening flight on the marshes, where you can meet the pinks and greys on their 'home ground'. There is no doubt that at times it is slightly unsporting to 'shoot them up' on the fields. It is inland that the really big bags are made and I do not think anyone really enjoys killing a lot of geese. The longer you have at the game the less you come to like this form of shooting. At the same time, it is sometimes the only way to come to terms, especially in unfavourable weather when you have dead-calm mornings, possibly with hard frost, when not a bird comes within range. A week of such weather can mean not a single goose in the bag, and this is serious when one has possibly only one week in the whole of the season.

This state of affairs was my lot a few years back, and towards the end of our stay I realized that if we did not tackle them on the fields we should go home empty handed.

There was one very large stubble within two miles of the shore where we noticed a strong 'feed' of pinks and greys. They had been coming to this stubble for three mornings and fed there until dusk, unless they were put off by farm-workers.

With some difficulty we persuaded the farmer to give us a morning there (at least Mac did the persuading, thereby earning a 'bonus'), and when the geese were absent in the afternoon we made a 'recce' of the ground.

The field was a very large one, bounded on three sides by dykes or 'pows'. The pows on north and south were full of water, that on the left was dry and there was plentiful cover from well-grown trees and brambles, indeed I have never seen a better place for hiding.

In addition, there was a very wet ditch which divided the field in the centre. Possibly at one time it had been another dyke, but it was partly filled in and in some places quite level.

It was far too shallow to form any cover unless one lay down quite flat, and some sort of top cover would have to be devised. Our plan was to conceal one gun in the dry dyke on the west side under the trees, and place two guns in this shallow trench and cover them with loose straw. Whether the geese would spot the new straw was the problem, and it was obvious that they would have to come fairly close before any shot could be taken, as it would be impossible to shoot from a lying position unless the birds came directly overhead. We also planned to put out two decoys (stuffed pinks) in the middle of the stubble. And we had to obtain some bales of straw from the cowman at the farm.

Early the next morning we sought out this cowman. We found him feeding his beasts in a great covered barn. Though it was an hour or so before the first streaks of dawn, we found him busy at his work.

He was a little gnome of a man with a wrinkled face and a broad grin. Surely we could have some straw, as much as we wanted! He climbed a ladder to the dim scented shadows above and descended with two generous bales.

When we reached the stack-yard it was still quite dark and the stars were shining. We left the van in the lee of some outbuildings and, burdened with our bales of straw, stuffed geese, and guns, we plodded out over the heavy plough towards our chosen field. There had been heavy rain the previous day and with every step our boots collected huge 'soles' of mud which made the walking very exhausting; that hateful plough seemed to go on for ever.

Plovers wailed sadly as we slowly toiled across, and from the east a cold wind blew, a wind which seemed to be rising. At last we saw the dim paleness of the stubble before us and with some difficulty (for it was still very dark) we located the shallow trench across the centre of the field.

I chose my place and Charles his, and when we lay down Mac covered us carefully with straw. We lay flat on our backs and, once down, it was surprising how sheltered we were. You had only to raise the head and at once you felt the cutting wind, which was now quite strong and threatened to blow away our covering.

When shooting in a 'lying ambush' like this, it is essential to see there is no large amount of straw *covering your gun*, otherwise, as soon as you make ready to shoot, you will find your sight obstructed by a mass of straw. The best way is to have the gun tucked into your side and only a few pieces of straw laid *lengthwise* along it, not across. It is essential, too, to have some sort of pillow to raise the head a little, and a log of wood served this purpose, well padded with straw.

After Mac had covered me, I heard him walking away across the field to cover Charles. Up above me the stars shone brightly, but already there was a faint greyness to the east and far away the farm cocks were hailing the new day.

Mac had not been gone more than five minutes when I was startled to see six geese passing low over me from the left. They came quite silently and their paddles were hanging. I believe I could have almost touched them with my gun as they sailed over me. Of course I was quite unprepared, for the first thing I knew was the hiss of the wind in their set, cupped wings. In a moment they had vanished, but I was sure they had come down on the stubble, probably not more than a hundred yards to my right.

This incident showed how dark it was, for Mac was at that

moment standing up and covering Charles not more than a hundred yards to my left! These early geese must have passed right over him, but neither Mac nor Charles had seen them, so they told me afterwards, nor apparently had the geese seen them.

We had arranged for Mac to give a single blast on his whistle when he saw geese coming, for of course from his hide in the dry pow he could command the whole field and the country to the south from which direction the birds were sure to come.

For a long time nothing happened, though it grew lighter all the time. Then mallard began passing out right over me, flock after flock, so low that I could have had some easy shooting. Two actually wheeled round and pitched very close to my ambush, for I heard them land.

Then I noticed gulls passing over, very high, flocks and flocks of gulls, all wandering inland with leisurely flight. A few green plover passed, and then the stars slowly faded, and it was day.

Not until the sun came over the hills did the geese begin to move from the sea. By that time the sky above me had changed from inky blue to pale blue and now it was a deep brilliant azure. The bright rays of the sun lit up the straw across my face, turning them into polished, golden-yellow masts. On each magnified stem there was a single, reflected dazzle from the bright rays. Passing gulls were now no longer silhouettes but pure white birds oaring along against a bright-blue background.

Then there came the whistle from the dyke and I knew Mac had seen the first lot of geese approaching. Soon I could hear their cackling, and a very big skein of pinks came wheeling round.

I lay very still under the straw and watched them pass directly overhead. Each bird was twisting its head sideways scanning the stubble. Some geese seemed to be dipping their necks and looking back at me under their tummies. But they were very cautious, and we had arranged not to fire unless the shot was certain.

They seemed very shy of the decoys and would not go near them, and at last they all came down with a forest of wagging wings at the far corner of the stubble.

Then I heard some cackling on my left, quite close, and through the straw could see a bunch of four, possibly a family party, dropping in. They were in easy range and I sat up, brushing away the cover with an unhurried motion. It is no easy matter to shoot 'sitting down', but at my shot one of the geese thumped the stubble. I should have had an easy right and left, but my second must have gone under the bird as the skein 'jumped' to my shot.

Mac then came across and took my place and, after covering him and taking his whistle, I went back to the tree dyke.

After half an hour we had several geese down and gathered— Charles had a right and left—all pinks. Then the sun went in and the wind increased in violence until it was blowing quite a gale. Added to this, rain began to drive down; bitter rain. What a change in a few hours!

Very soon we were wet through, lying out on the open field, and the 'cover' man was the only gun to avail himself of any shelter. Yet we stayed on, for the geese were still coming, and at last Mac ran out of cartridges and I had only three left. Charles also had shot himself out, so I gave him one case of BB. We all left the open hides and lined the dyke, and it was there I had the best shot of the day. I saw a big skein beating up for the trees in the teeth of the wind and rain, and it looked as though they would pass right over my tree.

There was an opening in the twigs on the left of the tree trunk, and I estimated that the leader would cross this loophole. I lifted the gun and was ready for him. In a split second his bill appeared on the right-hand side of the aperture and, swinging a little, I pressed the trigger. He dropped his head and slumped into a field of kale. My second shot took effect on the next in line and, though hard hit, he managed to keep up with the others.

But not for long. When we had almost lost sight of the skein in the driving rain, Mac saw one bird fall like a stone to the wet plough we had crossed at dawn, and when we struggled back to the shelter of the stacks we found him half-way across the wet furrows.

This successful morning made all the difference between success and failure, and that year we were able to go home with four geese apiece, this on our very last day when all chances of success had seemed hopeless.

Two golden rules must be observed when shooting on the fields in this fashion. See that you are lying quite flat and well covered, and never take any doubtful shot. Unless you let the birds come well in to you, you will miss again and again, for in your cramped posture there can be no easy swing. Each shot must be a 'sitter' if possible; I mean by that, of course, that the target should be flying within 25 or 30 yards of you. And it is necessary, also, to have your back to the wind. Geese alighting come into the wind and, if you are alert and ready, you can see them coming. Geese crossing behind you, however low, must be ignored, and even the crossing shot, if very close, had better be left alone. It takes about two seconds or a little more to sit up and fire; you have to get your 'sights' free of straw and to suppress all excitement. No easy thing when the birds are coming well!

22. 'Sawbath' Afternoon

ONE pouring wet 'Sawbath' afternoon Mac, Charles, and I were sitting by the fire at our H.Q. congratulating ourselves that it was a 'non-shooting' day. We had been out the day before at dawn and had had a gruelling time of it, lying out in the dykes in driving rain for four hours. Mac had been wet through and consequently he was now sitting with his jacket off, back to the fire, endeavouring to counteract the twinges of lumbago (incidentally incurring a heavy fine under our self-imposed rules).

Charles, replete as we all were with a good lunch, was soon fast asleep, and I wandered to the window and looked out over the flat 'goose fields' which stretched away to the shore of the firth a mile distant. They presented a sorry scene. All the previous day it had rained, all night as well; it had been raining since dawn. The gleaming floods lay out on the stubbles and the plough. Here and there black shocks of beans huddled drearily in sodden rows. I was watching a party of mallard disporting themselves in the flood water. They were enjoying themselves immensely. Some were swimming about, others preened, some were asleep with intucked, yellow bills. Through the powerful glasses I could make out every detail of their plumage, for the birds were not more than three hundred yards from our H.Q.

Now and again bursts of rain were flung against the window-panes and the last oak-leaves were spinning from the tree in the garden below. Then from out of the driving rain there came a skein of pinkfooted geese. They circled the plough and at last alighted in the centre of the stubble. There were about twenty birds in all, and I noticed the gaggle contained several young birds. For several minutes they stood erect and then, finding all was quiet, they began to feed, though in a cautious manner, stopping every now and then and scanning their immediate vicinity. When wild geese are at feed you will notice first one bird, then another, take this cautious survey of their surroundings—no set sentry is posted. It is a prolonged scrutiny. Those sharp, little, brown eyes are on the watch for every movement, and most of all for the sinister round knob of a man's head showing above the dyke.

In about ten minutes another party, a larger skein, came circling over. Seeing the other feeding geese, they alighted among them with a great outcry. This second skein comprised about thirty birds.

It is always fascinating to see them lowering with down-dropped paddles. At the moment of landing, the big grey wings wag vigorously and are then folded carefully. Every now and then (in rain) a feeding bird will shake itself like a dog and flap its wings, standing a-tiptoe as though to make sure that all is in order for instant flight.

Within the next hour geese arrived at intervals of ten minutes, until the whole stubble field in front of us was alive with them, possibly six or seven hundred birds. What a delight it was to watch them! The powerful glasses brought them very near, so that one could see every detail. We were most interested to see one of Peter Scott's 'marked' geese, with its behind dyed bright blue. This was one of the birds he had marked in the breeding grounds in Iceland the preceding summer.

The geese, as is their habit, were methodically working the field from end to end, but not coming very near a deep dyke which ran on two sides of the field. When feeding, they paced with a sprightly step quite unlike their domestic cousins.

Now and again two birds would fall out and run at each other with outstretched necks. At least two pairs were indulging in mild courtship.

Like the mallard, some began to play in the flooded furrows, drinking and splashing about. It was a wonderful scene and indeed a delightful way of spending a wet 'sawbath' afternoon. To be able to sit comfortably at one's window and watch these many beautiful birds feeding and playing, quite at ease, within a comparatively short distance from human habitation was quite entrancing. I was particularly interested to see what happened when dusk fell, for I knew the geese would not stay there after dark.

Very soon a vast flock of crows and daws came cawing over the feeding geese, circling low over their backs and causing them great uneasiness. But presently all the black, mischievous birds (who were obviously out to tease the geese) alighted at the far end of the stubble and began feeding busily towards the main flock. The geese did not like this at all, and as the hundreds of rooks and daws, looking like so many busy black-beetles, moved along the field, they turned about and walked away, feeding as they went.

I saw one rook fly up and try to settle on the back of one of the pinks, which turned round and hissed fiercely at it.

The rooks did not feed for long, and I was glad, for I feared they might drive all the geese away and I should not be able to watch the moment of the 'jump'.

As it grew dusk I noticed that more and more birds had their heads up. They seemed increasingly restless and vigilant. Just when I thought they were about to jump, however, down went their heads again, and they were feeding as busily as before, though of course some still kept a strict watch.

Then I noticed that all the birds at the far end of the field were standing stock still with upraised heads, a perfect forest of necks. They were evidently 'going'. By now the autumn dusk was far advanced, so much so that I could barely make out the geese in my glasses.

Then at last the outermost birds jumped, and the whole lot lifted in a wave, crying all together. Away they went into the mists over the firth and our most entertaining afternoon was over.

That actual moment of the 'lift' comes when visibility is becoming really poor, when some enemy might be able to creep up on them unawares, for geese have not good sight at night, no better than that of rooks.

I do not think there is any given signal from any particular bird: it is an urge or impulse which affects every bird at the same moment.

The ways of wildfowl are always full of mystery and charm. We know roughly their habits, but, even so, there comes a time when we find ourselves at a loss to explain certain actions. And what affects wildfowl also affects the gulls, which are always found beside the Highland firths. On some nights they all come in low, bank high, in ghostly mobs, half-seen in the twilight. And all fly in the same direction.

There may be no wind to cause them to fly low, yet every lot one sees fly at the same altitude, hedge high. On another evening they will all come in high, so high that you can barely see them. I do not believe it is always the choice of feeding ground which influences altitude.

As a general rule you will notice that all wildfowl at morning or evening flight will adopt the same line and altitude. One evening all the geese may fly up the firth, on another they will go in the opposite direction. No doubt tide and wind have a lot to do with it, but the strange thing is that every bird has the same idea and at flight time every bunch which comes in will do the same things.

On most firths there are big sand-banks and these form the sleeping-places for the geese and ducks. High or low water, the geese go out just the same and are carried hither and thither by the action of the tides.

If geese are sitting opposite to you at morning flight, it does not always mean the chance of a shot. I would rather have them well to right or left of my ambush, for it is not often they fly straight in unless the wind is strong and it is blowing directly from you to them. Even so, they usually tack a little to left or right when they make for the shore at dawn.

One of the charms about estuary shooting, apart from the varying habits of the fowl, is the ever-changing bird population. These estuaries are like great railway stations in our human world, or perhaps airports would be a better simile. One morning you may see thousands of lapwings and few geese. On another, vast flocks of golden plover. Here today and gone tomorrow, the multitudes of travellers arrive and pass on.

There surely is the inmost lure of wildfowling. Always you can watch, if you have an observant eye, the comings and goings of these feathered travellers. Theirs is no confined and petty life, they can roam, endlessly, the skyways of the world.

23. Dawn Ambush Inland

THE conical, neat stacks in the farm-yard were black, peaked silhouettes against the sky as we brought the shooting-brake to a standstill and disembarked. Stars trembled bright and clear overhead. From the farm buildings came sounds of the day's work already begun, lowing of cattle, the bang of a door, clatter of buckets. Here and there a lantern glowed on beam and plaster; there was a sense of cosiness in the enclosed yards which smelt of warm hay and cows. This was a regular haven for rats, mice, sparrows, finches, robins, tits, and men. So does each winter dawn follow a pattern on these northern farms. Winter after winter it must be the same: lights springing up in bothy and farm-house, hobnailed boots clumping on the frosty, ridged mud, or rustling in last summer's harvest of sweet hay and straw. I cannot picture these steadings in high summer.

A labourer emerged from a doorway carrying a swinging lantern which gave him an old-world look. On his back was a great truss of hay. He vanished into another dimly-lit doorway.

Beside it, through a square aperture in the wall, just large enough to allow a beast's head to look through, a great bull blinked at us under wrinkled brows.

But away from the bustle and security of this northern 'Scherm', far out on those flat, rich fields where no tree or bank could break the wind, night still reigned supreme.

A shadow hurrying off was a hare disturbed from the frozen furrow, and the dim white lines of snow which lay between each plough scar were clearly visible in the darkness. Green plover wailed mournfully on our right, and we even heard a snipe rise as we staggered over the frozen ploughland. It was beastly walking, enough to wrench one's 'guts' out, for we carried a heavy burden. Mac, Charles, and I each bore upon our backs a vast truss of straw in addition to our guns, cartridges, and six stuffed decoys.

I have short legs and soon fell behind. Mac and Charles vanished in the gloom, though I could hear them muttering, and the clump of their rubber boots died away.

The field seemed never ending. I was soon tramping as if in a dream, stars overhead, white furrows below, and now and again the faint, thin cries of birds roused from sleep or hurrying seawards. For it was that time when the mallard leave their night grounds for the coast. 'Quack! quack! quack!' again and again, I heard one spring up and wing away for the distant firth, though the bird itself was quite invisible. Sometimes too, as I tramped along, I heard the keen, faint whicker of ducks' wings passing directly over head accompanied by the muted stuttering quacks, the same sounds one hears at night when the mallard are going inshore.

Something took shape in the blank wall ahead and resolved itself into the spread, fan-shaped branches of a hedgerow oak. Beneath it I made out Charles and Mac, who were waiting for me.

Mac was to act as 'cover man' and Charles and I were to go out into the stubble where there was a shallow dyke, mercifully dry, as I would not have relished a wet bed on such a wintry morning. Actually the ground itself was not wet as the frost had been fairly hard, but I made sure that much of the straw which fell to my share was used to form a bed to lie upon.

Having covered up Charles and myself, Mac vanished in the direction of the oak-trees, and I was left with a sense of loneliness. Only the wind, a cruel wind like a sharp sword, rustled in the straw which covered me. I lay on my back with a light covering over my face, gun between my knees. Fifty yards down wind of me Mac had placed the decoys, though I could not of course see them from where I lay.

The sky was a little lighter, though the stars still burned brightly, and now and again the dark shapes of mallard sped overhead. All these things, the snug farm-yard, the sound and movements of fowl, the slowly growing day, all were a part of my pleasure, a pleasure as keen as the actual shooting and sight of the geese which we hoped would come. Bands of larks began to twitter somewhere close at hand and, in a short while, two of them actually settled on the straw which covered me.

Then quickly the night drained from the sky and the savage, wintry scene grew visible. Naked oaks (with spring so far away) lining that distant hedge, the snow-striped stubble, the withered sedge along the ridge of my shallow dyke. Some stems bore pennants of dead leaf, which fluttered and bowed in the cruel wind.

Green plover came over me in big flocks, their rounded wings beating like ping-pong bats. A hare was visible far out on the stubble. By twisting my head sideways I could see her with the wind blowing her fur. She hopped about nibbling, now here, now there, and then came at a shambling canter directly for my hide. Five feet away she stopped, with eyes wide and questioning, long whiskers working as her nose fluttered up and down.

She caught some taint on the air and was suspicious. But how I enjoyed the intimate 'close-up' of her, this wild Highland hare!

A strange life she led on these wide fields, a companion of the wild, grey geese, her only enemy the lurking grieve or 'horraman' crouching in some ditch on a Saturday afternoon. The farmers thereabouts do not seem to be fond of the gun and, anyway, they are concerned with making money and not with sport.

After a long scrutiny of my hide, she turned about and hurried off, her posterior rocking up and down as she made off. She ran past Charles whom I could now see as a slightly raised hump of straw a hundred yards down the dyke.

There was a bunch of withered thistles close by, and to these came a starveling blue tit. It searched each shabby head and seemed to find some seeds, for it was busy there for five minutes before flying off. How frail it looked with the searing wind ruffling its tiny body!

Looking at this solitary thistle I was reminded of a story which Charles had told me the night before as we sat toasting our toes before the fire at H.Q.

During the first German war he was ordered to attack a wood where German machine-gunners were entrenched. It was an ugly proposition and his men did not like it any more than did Charles. But in due course they made for this wood in 'short rushes' and the German machine-gunners began to find their mark.

A thump and a grunt, a thump and a groan—man after man rolled over as they crossed that field of death. Some shivered and lay still; others rolled and kicked like mortally stricken rabbits.

The only cover Charles could see ahead of him was a solitary, dead thistle, and he felt, if he reached this, all would be well. He did so and lay down, and he told me it was wonderful how that frail, dead weed seemed to give confidence.

The German machine-gunners and snipers in the wood were busy. But when they saw the thistle they changed to another target. It was only a thistle, not a man, and so Charles lived. So it came about that nearly forty years afterwards he was lying up the dyke above me.

Actually, with the incredible luck that some men seem to have in war, he came through the '14–'18 war without a scratch, and even the latter end of the recent world war was survived without a wound of any sort. But I thought to myself (thinking over this story of the thistle), that in war the man who has learnt how to take cover has an advantage over the other man who knows nothing of fieldcraft. No one can guard against the haphazard shell or mortar which cannot be avoided, but when you are up against a man with a rifle and machine-gun who is seeking for you, field-craft is of immense help, as any regular infantryman will tell you.

I seem to have digressed from this account of a morning ambush; the reader must forgive me.

The sky to the east was now a clear yellow over the firth, shading to duck-egg green at the skies' zenith. Huge, sombre snow-clouds were rolling westwards, the lights in the farm went out, and gulls came over in a ceaseless procession, each birdy brain steering an unerring course. Flakes of snow began to fly past horizontally and the brightness in the sky to the east was dimmed in a grey curtain.

Then, from the line of oaks, came Mac's shrill whistle which told he had seen geese. My thumb slid the safety-catch from safe to ready.

I heard their faint cries for a minute or so before I saw the skein, a small knot of pinks hanging apparently motionless against the flying snowflakes. They circled in, cackling and setting their wings, but for some reason they did not like the look of the decoys, and after six or seven circuits made off with that sudden quickening of wing-beats which tells of minds made up.

The next lot was a big pack of pinks which passed right over high and never looked like coming to us, but the flight really got under weigh and parties were circling our flanking fields, and it was only a matter of time before one lot chose our stubble.

Six greys did so ten minutes later and passing low over Charles gave him an easy right and left, both birds hitting the snow 'bump, bump' among the decoys.

I never had a shot, and at 10 a.m. we packed up. It is amazing how frozen toes and fingers and no more sights or sounds of geese can quickly damp the enthusiasm of the most enthusiastic fowler!

Yet how I had enjoyed it all! Each little incident: the hare, the tit on the withered thistle, the sense of bitter winter on these starved and frozen fields!

So does the true fowler taste of the inward charm of his sport. It is the natural scene: the beauty of a northern winter dawn, the blazing sunset sky reflected across the quiet firth at evening, the silent majesty of a night of stars with the faint, unearthly cries of wildfowl moving on their mysterious journeyings, which mean so much.

Some insensitive persons call this sort of thing 'blah', but *Dark Estuary* has not been written for insensitive people whose main object is the butchering of wildfowl and getting tipsy in the local pub.

Those who have known the call of the wild tides in the lonely places know better. And each winter that call will come again and again, perhaps for as long as life lasts.

APPENDIX

Wildfowling Terms

Barnies	Barnacle geese
Blackbacks	Black-backed gulls
Black Duck (also Mussel Duck)	Scoter
Black Geese	Brent and Barnacles
Brants	Brent geese
Brew	Marsh edge
Cover Man	The man who covers the stubble man
'Coys	Goose decoys, usually stuffed wild geese
Cripple Stopper	The 12-bore carried by the puntsman
Dunbirds	Dunlin (this also applies to other small waders on the coast)
Dyke	A creek in fowler's parlance
The Ebb	Receding tide
Flighting	Shooting wildfowl at dawn and late evening
The Flow	Advancing or 'making' tide
Gaggle	A collection of geese on the ground
Greys	Greylag geese
Gutter	A creek
Gutty Boots	Long, rubber wading-boots
Half-Curlew	Whimbrel
Half-Snipe	Jack Snipe
Harnser	Heron
Hoodie	Hooded Crow
Knot	A small, edible, wading bird
Long Case Cartridge	3-inch cartridge
Magnum	A 3-inch case, 12-bore gun fully choked
Ox birds	Dunlin
Oystercock Pie	Wildfowl pie
Pensioner	A fowl crippled by shot
Pinks	Pinkfooted geese
Plickplack	The mud on the tide's edge
Pow	Ditch
Pricked Goose	Wounded Goose
Puit	Black-headed Gull
Punting	Gun-punting to fowl

163

Reddy	Redshank
Sawbills	Gooseanders and Mergansers
Scotch Goose	Brent or Greylag
Sea Pies	Oyster-catchers
Setting Board	Hand paddles used in the punt
Shellies	Shelduck
Shovel Bill	Shoveller
Sit Bag	The large, canvas game-bag stuffed with a folded mackintosh which serves as a fowler's seat
Skein	A collection of geese in the air
Spring of Teal	Teal in flight
Stubble Man	The gun ambushing out in the field
Strath	Mountain valley
Summer Snipe	Common Sandpiper
Team of Duck	Ducks in flight
Whisp of Snipe	Snipe in flight
Whoopers	Whooper Swans
Woodcock Owl	Short-eared Owl